Also by Julia Child

Mastering the Art of French Cooking, Volume I
(with Simone Beck and Louisette Bertholle)

The French Chef Cookbook

Mastering the Art of French Cooking, Volume II
(with Simone Beck)

From Julia Child's Kitchen

The Way to Cook

Cooking with Master Chefs

In Julia's Kitchen with Master Chefs

Julia's Menus for Special Occasions

Julia's Menus for Special Occasions

by Julia Child

In collaboration with E. S. Yntema

Photographs by James Scherer

Alfred A. Knopf   New York   1998

This Is a Borzoi Book
Published by Alfred A. Knopf, Inc.

The recipes in this book were originally published in the
books *Julia Child & Company* and *Julia Child & More
Company,* which were published by Alfred A. Knopf,
Inc., in 1978 and 1979 respectively. Copyright © 1978
(*Julia Child & Company*) and copyright © 1979 (*Julia
Child & More Company*) by Julia Child. These two
books were also released in a single edition as *Julia
Child's Menu Cookbook,* published in 1991 by Wings
Books, distributed by Outlet Book Company, Inc., a
Random House Company, by arrangement with Alfred
A. Knopf, Inc.

"Lo-Cal Banquet" and "Birthday Dinner" both
appeared in somewhat shorter form in *McCall's.*

Library of Congress Cataloging-in-Publication Data
Child, Julia.
Julia's menus for special occasions / by Julia Child in
collaboration with E. S. Yntema ; photographs by
James Scherer. — 1st ed.
p.   cm.
Includes index.
ISBN 0-375-40338-8
1. Entertaining.   2. Menus.   3. Cookery.   I. Yntema,
E. S.   II. Title.
TX731.C544   1998
642'.4—dc21   98-6374
                                          CIP

Manufactured in the United States of America
First Edition

Contents

Acknowledgments

This is a book of menus drawn from our television series *Julia Child & Company* and its sequel, *Julia Child & More Company*. The recipes for the complete series appeared in two separate books, were then all collected into one big book, and are now split into four convenient smaller books, of which this is the second volume.

The series was produced for public television at WGBH TV in Boston, with Russell Morash as producer/director in association with Ruth Lockwood. The food designer and recipe developer was Rosemary Manell, who worked closely with our photographer, James Scherer. Marian Morash, chef for the popular *This Old House*, was also executive chef for us. I count us fortunate indeed to have had E. S. Yntema as a writer. Peggy Yntema's wit and spirit always make for good reading.

It takes a peck of people to put on shows such as these, and other members of our team at one time or another included Gladys Christopherson, Bess Coughlin, Wendy Davidson, Bonnie Eleph, Jo Ford, Temi Hyde, Sara Moulton, Pat Pratt, John Reardon, Bev Seamons, and, of course, our able makeup artist, Louise Miller. I have not mentioned the technicians, camera crew, and lighting engineers, or our book designer, Chris Pullman, or our favorite editor at Knopf, Judith Jones.

Introduction

What are you going to do when half of your dinner guests are strict vegetarians, or when you need a menu for a group on a very low-calorie diet regime, or when you want to give a high-class cocktail party, or when you'd like an expandable menu for one of those evenings where 20 guests may expand to 30? You'll have to make detailed shopping lists for any of these events. And how about equipment? What can you prepare in advance, what can you freeze, how long does it take to make each dish, and what should you serve anyway? Maybe you need help! And that is what this book is here to do.

Taking the low-calorie meal as an example, you certainly don't want anything at your table to look or taste like dismal diet food. Everyone is to admire and enjoy it, and in fact no one should even suspect your intentions, from pre-dinner drinks through caramel-crowned apple dessert. The main course is a fragrant and sumptuous Mediterranean bouillabaisse of chicken, giving a clear signal to those in the know that you, by the way, are a genuine member of the "in" group, since that style of cooking is definitely chic. Even more "in" but equally delicious as well, is the accompanying bowl of its traditional deep-pink garlic sauce, its *rouille,* which is passed separately so one can take as much— or as little—as one wishes.

The chapter starts with a lively discussion of its subject plus a few useful hints. It lists the marketing and storage of ingredients and staples, then launches into the shrimp and green bean appetizer, and gives complete directions for the chicken, including how to pre-cook it the day before and finish it the day of. A column suggests the timing schedule for the event, another offers variations on the menu, a third gives ideas on what to do with leftovers, and a postscript computes the calorie count.

There! The whole menu and all its parts are laid out for you in very do-able detail, which is true for all the menus in the book. No impossible-to-find food items, no outrageous utensils. All the dishes described here are carefully designed for the home chef who loves to cook, and who wants to serve splendid meals to people who love to eat.

Have a good time with them, and
Toujours bon appétit!
Julia Child
1998

♪   *indicates stop here*
▼   *indicates further discussion under Remarks*

Julia's Menus for Special Occasions

A menu designed around duck, with a special roasting method which guarantees perfect cooking and easy carving. Herewith, also, a sumptuous apricot and hazelnut cake.

Birthday Dinner

Whenever anyone asks me what I want for a birthday dinner, I always say, "Roast duck and a big gooey cake." I love to eat duck when the skin is crisp and mahogany red-brown, the legs and wings just tender through, the breast meat moist, rosy, and tender. And guests always feel it's a special treat. You don't see duck too often at dinner parties. It does pose problems, and I've been giving them some thought.

Even a carver as adept as my husband finds that the docile duck becomes as stubborn as an ostrich on the carving board; that's the first problem. Second is the fact that roasted the usual way the breast meat is done much sooner than the leg and wing. Fat is problem number three: for perfect flavor, the fat must be drained off during cooking. But if you want a crisp skin, you can't cook it in the normal manner because the meat will be overdone. Many a cook is resigned to ruining the meat in order to enjoy a crackling skin.

A famous Chinese solution to these problems is Peking duck, the glory of Mandarin cuisine, for which one starts way ahead by forcing air between the duck's skin and flesh and hanging up the inflated carcass to dry. For the fine Norman ducks of Rouen, which are a cross between wild and domestic strains and are sold unbled, the French have thought up the duck press and produce a carnal feast indeed. Here the partly roasted bird is peeled of its skin, the breast is carved, the legs and wings are removed, and the carcass is crushed for its juices. The breast is then warmed in these juices, a rich dark red, laced with Burgundy wine. The legs and wings finish cooking while you eat the more delicate breast, and they come in as an encore. This requires expert servers, a chafing dish, and a duck press. But when we filmed the process at the Dorin brothers' restaurant in Rouen, I also showed a less elaborate alternative. With that in mind, I decided to continue with the roast-peel idea that I used then to produce another and simpler dish.

This way of dealing with duck involves neither sideboard antics nor fancy paraphernalia; and it solves all three of the problems I mentioned. The duck can be beautifully presented, since it is carved in the kitchen, and served before its redolence evaporates. I like to contrast its rich flavor, crisp skin, and succulent meat with a velvety purée of parsnips. Their very special flavor, earthy and sweetish—so compatible with duck—is transformed by puréeing. People who think they don't like parsnips are almost always enchanted with them this way, wondering happily, "What can it be?" I like to serve the parsnip purée in baked zucchini shells—chosen for their unobtrusive taste and their jade-and-emerald color—an easy and elegant vegetable accompaniment. I'd hate to disturb the rapport of these congenial flavors with anything else, so I serve another vegetable as a separate course.

Like opposite primary and secondary colors, fruit flavors seem to balance duck. So I've chosen a fruit-layered cake for the birthday dessert: crisp strips of nut meringue spread with a luscious apricot filling flavored with orange liqueur and a touch of Cognac, plus a discreet amount of butter cream, just enough to mediate the contrast in taste and texture.

I like this luxurious menu; and I also like to feel rested as well as hospitable when I call my best friends in to the table. No damp brow or hot hands for the birthday cook! I prepare most of this very posh dinner well in advance, and the work itself isn't difficult. The gorgeous cake is not only more fun to make than the sponge-layer kind, it's easier. And in the privacy of my kitchen, nobody can see me subduing the duck.

Preparations

Marketing and Storage:
Staples to have on hand

Salt
Peppercorns
Sugar (both granulated and confectioners)
Pure vanilla extract
Almond extract
Cream of tartar
Stick cinnamon
Bay leaves
Thyme or sage
Mustard (the strong Dijon type or Düsseldorf) ▼
Apricot preserves or jam (optional)
All-purpose flour
Olive oil and cooking oil
Wines and liqueurs: dry white French vermouth, Cognac or rum, dry Port or Sercial Madeira, orange or apricot liqueur
Vegetables and fruits: a few carrots, onions, shallots or scallions, an orange, and lemons
Eggs (12)
Cream (½ pint [225 g] or so)
Fresh bread crumbs (in the freezer) ▼

Specific ingredients for this menu

Crab (enough for 6 as a first course; see recipe) ▼
Ducklings (two 4- to 5-pound or 2- to 2½-kg) ▼
Zucchini (6, about 6 inches or 15 cm long)
Parsnips (1½ to 2 pounds or ¾ to 1 kg)
Broccoli (2 bunches)
Parsley (1 bunch; or 1 or 2 of watercress)
Unsalted butter (about 1 pound or 450 g)
Dried apricots (1 pound or 450 g)
Whole shelled hazelnuts and blanched almonds (about 4 ounces or 120 g of each) ▼
Shaved (thinly sliced) almonds, toasted (about 8 ounces or 240 g)

▶ *Remarks:*

Staples

Mustard: always store prepared mustard in the refrigerator, otherwise it goes off in flavor; most supermarkets carry several varieties of strong European-type mustard, and the ballpark variety is not meant here. *Bread crumbs:* it's useful to have these always on hand in the freezer, and crumbs from fresh bread are best. To make them easily, cut crusts off nonsweet white bread, such as French, Italian, and Viennese, and crumb either in the blender or with the grating disk of a food processor; store in a plastic bag in the freezer where they will keep for weeks.

Specific ingredients for this menu

Crab: if you buy frozen crab, allow a day for it to defrost in the refrigerator, and see notes on crab in "Fish Talk," page 29. *Ducks:* frozen ducks, like all frozen poultry, should be defrosted in the refrigerator to minimize juice loss since too quick defrosting can cause the ice crystals to pierce the flesh. Your best alternative is to defrost them in a sinkful of water. In either case, leave ducks in their plastic wrapping, and allow 2 to 3 days in the refrigerator, several hours in water. *Hazelnuts and almonds:* nuts are perishable, especially hazelnuts (called filberts by some people); taste them to be sure they are fresh, and store them in the freezer. To skin hazelnuts, place in a roasting pan in a 350°F/180°C oven, tossing about every 5 minutes or so, for 15 to 20 minutes, or until the nuts are lightly browned; rub in a towel to remove as much skin as you easily can. Toasting also gives them added flavor. Toast whole blanched shaved almonds in the same manner.

Chesapeake Lump Crabmeat Appetizer

Since how much you season your crabmeat depends entirely on its quality, I can only make suggestions. Freshly boiled crabmeat needs nothing on it, I think, only lemon, salt, and a peppermill passed at the table, and to each his own. Frozen and canned crab are very much up to you and your tastebuds as you fix your appetizer. Lemon juice, certainly, and often you will need very finely minced shallot or scallion, sometimes a little minced celery, and fresh minced dill or fragrant bottled dill weed, plus salt and pepper, and perhaps a tossing with good olive oil; I like to pass mayonnaise separately, for those who wish it. Arrange the crab on a bed of either shredded lettuce or romaine, or surround it with watercress, or wreathe it in seasoned ripe tomato pulp or red pimiento. You could also include quartered hard-boiled eggs, but that would be dictated by how much crab you were serving per person—and since crab is a luxury, ⅓ cup (¾ dL) for each guest is generous enough, even for a birthday party.

Roast Duck with Cracklings

In this method, the duck is given a preliminary or partial roasting, then a skin peeling and carving; half an hour before serving, the legs finish cooking along with the skin, cut into strips which render their fat and crisp in the oven. The breast meat is warmed briefly in wine and seasonings just before being arranged on the platter with the browned legs and crackling skin. All but the final cooking may be done in advance.

For 6 people
Two 4- to 5-pound (2- to 2¼-kg) ducklings
1 Tb cooking oil
1 medium-size carrot, roughly chopped
1 medium-size onion, roughly chopped
Salt, thyme or sage, 1 bay leaf, ½ cup (1 dL) strong prepared mustard, Dijon type
Generous 1 cup (¼ L) lightly pressed down, fresh nonsweet white bread crumbs
2 Tb duck-roasting fat or melted butter
1 Tb minced shallots or scallions
Pepper
¼ cup (½ dL) or so dry Port or Sercial Madeira

Preliminaries to roasting

Chop the ducks' wings off at the elbows and brown them in cooking oil with the neck, gizzard, and vegetables, in a heavy saucepan, then simmer in water to cover and ½ teaspoon salt for an hour. Drain, degrease, and reserve liquid for sauce later; you should have about ½ cup (1 dL) strong meaty liquid.

Meanwhile, here's a good trick for easy carving (you won't be carving at table with this recipe, but it still makes the duck easier to disjoint): working from inside the duck, sever ball joints where wings join shoulders (as illustrated opposite, top left) and second joints join small of back (opposite, lower left). Again for easy carving, remove wishbone from inside of neck opening and add to duck stock.

Sprinkle inside of duck with ¼ teaspoon salt and a pinch of thyme or sage, and tuck in the bay leaf. Pull out any loose fat from inside neck and cavity. Prick the skin all over on the back and sides (where you see the yellow fat under the skin) with a sharp-pronged fork or trussing needle, but do not go too deep where rosy flesh shows through skin, or the duck juices will seep out and stain the skin as the duck is roasting. To truss the duck, first, push needle through carcass underneath the wings, then come up around one wing, catch the neck skin flap against the backbone (upper right picture); come out over opposite wing, and tie. For the second truss (middle right picture), push needle through underside of drumstick ends, catching the tail piece as you go, come back over tops of drumsticks, and tie. The neatly trussed duck will look like the one in the bottom picture.

🕐 May be prepared for roasting a day in advance.

A preliminary roasting

Preheat oven to 350°F/180°C. Place ducks breast up in roasting pan and set in middle level of preheated oven. Roast 30 to 35 minutes, or until breast meat is just springy to the touch (rather than squashy like raw duck)—this means the breast meat is just rosy and easy to carve, but the legs and thighs (which will cook more later) are still rare.

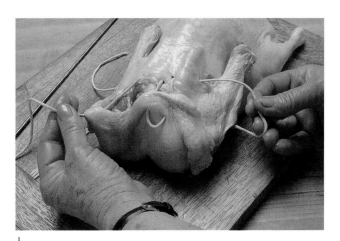

↓

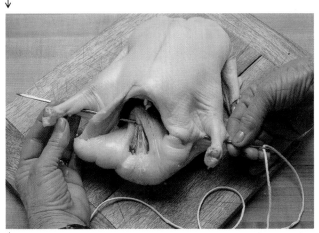

↓

↓

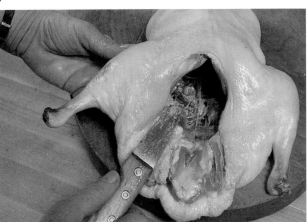

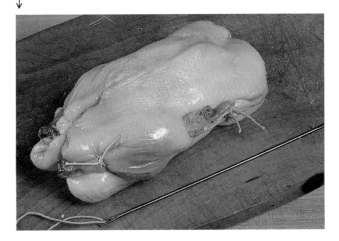

Skinning and carving—preliminaries to final cooking

While the duck is still warm, peel off its skin as follows: cut a slit down the length of the duck on either side of the breastbone, as I've done in the picture below, and remove skin from breast and thighs.

Then cut up the duck as shown in the lower right picture. Remove leg-thigh sections and separate legs from thighs; peel as much skin off them as you easily can, and cut off visible fat. Cut fat and skin into strips ¼ inch (¾ cm) wide and place in a baking dish. Paint legs and thighs with a thin coating of mustard, roll in crumbs, and arrange in another baking dish; sprinkle tops with a dribble of duck-roasting fat or melted butter.

Film a frying pan (not of cast iron) with duck fat or melted butter, sprinkle in half the shallots or scallions, carve the breast meat into neat slices, as illustrated, and arrange in the pan. Season lightly with salt and pepper and sprinkle with the remaining shallots or scallions. Pour in the Port or Madeira and the duck stock from the first paragraph. (You may wish to roast the carcasses and wings—which have little meat—a few minutes more and save for the cook's lunch the next day; that's what I do, at least.)

🕐 May be prepared to this point several hours before serving.

Finishing the ducks

Preheat the oven to 400°F/200°C, and half an hour before you plan to serve dinner, set dishes with crumbed legs and thighs and skin strips in the upper third level. Roast skin until the pieces have browned nicely and rendered their fat; remove with a slotted spoon to a plate covered with paper toweling to drain; then toss with a sprinkling of salt and pepper. Roast legs until just tender when pressed—about 20 to 25 minutes. Keep both warm in turned-off oven, door ajar, until you are ready to serve. Between courses, as you are changing plates, bring the pan with the duck breast slices barely to the simmer, to poach the meat but keep it the color of a deep blush. Then arrange it on a hot platter and rapidly boil down the cooking juices until syrupy while you arrange the legs and the skin cracklings on the platter; pour the reduced pan juices over the breast meat and serve at once.

Remarks:

I was discussing duck the other day with a restaurant owner who serves a lot of duck to his clientele. He says he puts his in a 250°F/130°C oven and lets them roast slowly for 3 or 4 hours, pricking them several times to drain out the fat. The meat emerges a nice medium rare, the birds exude a lot of fat, and when he is ready to serve he pops them back in the oven, at 550°F/290°C, to brown and crisp the skin. I haven't tried the final crisping, since I fear so hot an oven and its effect on the rosy meat, but the slow roast is certainly easy and painless.

Purée of Parsnips

*To go with roast duck, goose, pork,
or turkey*

*For 4 to 6 servings (more than you need
for the zucchini boats, but the purée is so
good and reheats so well, I am suggest-
ing almost double the necessary amount)*

2 pounds (1 kg) parsnips

Salt

5 Tb cream

2 Tb butter

Pepper

Trim and peel the parsnips and cut into slices
about ⅓ inch (1 cm) thick. Place in a saucepan
with water barely to cover and a teaspoon of
salt. Bring to the boil, cover pan, and boil
slowly 20 to 30 minutes or until parsnips are
tender and water has almost entirely evaporated.
Using a vegetable mill or food processor,
purée, and return to saucepan. Beat in the
cream and butter, and season to taste with salt
and pepper. Set pan in another containing simmering water, cover, and let cook 20 to 30
minutes more—note the subtle change in taste
that takes place. Correct seasoning before
serving.

🕐 May be cooked in advance and reheated
over simmering water.

Zucchini Boats

*To hold a purée of parsnips or other
cooked filling*

**6 zucchini of uniform size, about 6 inches
(15 cm) long**

Salt

2 to 3 Tb melted butter

Pepper

Trim stem ends off zucchini and cut zucchini in
half lengthwise. Hollow out the centers with a
grapefruit knife, leaving a 3/16-inch (scant ¾-
cm) border of flesh all around. (Save removed
centers for soup.) Drop the boat-shaped zucchini in a large pan of lightly salted boiling
water and boil slowly 4 to 5 minutes, or until
barely tender—they must hold their shape.
Brush with melted butter, season lightly with
salt and pepper, and arrange in a roasting pan.
Shortly before serving, pour in ¼ inch (¾ cm)
water, and bake 4 to 5 minutes in the upper
third of a preheated 425°F/220°C oven—to
give them a little more flavor, but without letting them overcook and lose their shape.

Assembling

Arrange the hot zucchini boats in a serving
dish, and with a pastry bag and cannelated
tube, rapidly pipe the hot parsnip purée into
them—much more attractive than when they
are filled with a spoon. Serve at once.

Broccoli Flowerettes

*For 6 people have a good 2 quarts or 2
liters of prepared broccoli— 1 ½ bunches*

This doesn't need a full-scale recipe, since
broccoli is so easy to cook, but for the freshest-
tasting, greenest, slightly crunchy, beautiful
broccoli, you do have to peel the stems. Then
the broccoli cooks in less than 5 minutes.
Here's how to go about it: cut the stems off the
broccoli, leaving the bud ends about 2½
inches (6½ cm) long; quarter the bud ends to
make them all about 3/16 inch (scant ¾ cm) in
diameter. From the cut end, pull off the skin up
to the bud section. Peel the stems with a knife,
going down to the tender white. Refrigerate in
a covered bowl until you are ready to cook the
broccoli.

To cook, you may blanch the broccoli
ahead, and plunge into boiling water just
before serving; or boil between courses, since it
cooks so quickly. Bring a very large kettle with
5 to 6 quarts or liters lightly salted water to the
rapid boil, drop in the broccoli, cover the
kettle, and bring to the boil again over highest
heat; as soon as the water boils, remove cover
and boil slowly 4 to 5 minutes, just until broccoli is cooked through, slightly crunchy, and a
beautiful bright green. Remove at once from
the boiling water—a large perforated scoop is
useful here. If you are serving immediately,
arrange quickly on a platter, seasoning lightly
with salt and pepper, the Brown Butter Sauce
(see following recipe)—or use melted butter—
and drops of lemon juice. (Or you may pre-
cook the broccoli until barely tender before
dinner and spread it out on a towel to cool rapidly; keep a kettle of fresh salted water at the
boil between courses, and plunge the broccoli
into the boiling water just before serving, to
reheat for a moment; then dress it on the platter as described.)

Brown Butter Sauce:
For 6 servings
Cut 1 stick (4 ounces or 1 1 5 g) butter into
fairly thin slices—for even melting—and place
in a small saucepan over moderate heat, bringing the butter to a boil. Skim off foam as it
collects and cook until butter turns a nice nutty
brown—this will take only 2 to 3 minutes in
all. If serving immediately, spoon over the
food, leaving speckled particles in bottom of
pan. For later serving, spoon into a clean pan
and either reheat or keep over hot water.

The Los Gatos Gâteau Cake

A Dacquoise type of apricot-filled torte

For a 12-by-4-inch cake about 2 inches high, serving 12 to 14

The Meringue-Nut Layers:

¾ cup (1⅓ dL) each toasted and skinned hazelnuts and blanched toasted almonds

1 cup (¼ L) sugar

¾ cup (1¾ dL or 5 to 6) egg whites

Pinch salt and ¼ tsp cream of tartar

3 Tb additional sugar

1 Tb pure vanilla extract

¼ tsp almond extract

Equipment

A blender or food processor; 2 pastry sheets about 12 by 15 inches (30 x 37 cm) each (nonstick recommended); a 14-inch (35-cm) pastry bag with ½-inch (1½-cm) tip opening (recommended); a flexible-blade spatula

Using a blender or food processor, pulverize the hazelnuts with half the sugar, then the almonds with the remaining sugar. Preheat oven to 250°F/120°C, placing racks in upper and lower third levels. Butter and flour the pastry sheets, and trace 4 rectangles on them 12 by 4 inches (30 x 10 cm), as I have done here.

Beat the egg whites at slow speed until they have foamed, then beat in the salt and cream of tartar; increase speed gradually to fast, and beat until egg whites form stiff shining peaks. Immediately sprinkle in the remaining 3 tablespoons sugar while beating, add the vanilla and almond extracts, and continue for 30 seconds more. Remove beater from stand and at once sprinkle on the pulverized nuts and sugar, folding them in rapidly with a rubber spatula as you do so. Scoop the meringue into the pastry bag and squeeze out onto the traced rectangles, starting at the edges of each and

working inward; smooth with a flexible-blade spatula. (Or spread and smooth with a spatula.) Set in oven and bake about an hour, switching levels every 20 minutes or so. The meringue layers are done when you can gently push them loose; do not force them, since they break easily and will budge only when they are ready to do so. Remove to a rack.

🕐 If not used within an hour or so, keep in a warming oven at 120°F/50°C, or wrap airtight and freeze.

The Apricot Filling:
About 2½ cups (6 dL)

1 pound (450 g) dried apricots

1 cup (¼ L) dry white French vermouth

2 cups (½ L) water

1 stick cinnamon

Zest (colored part of peel) of 1 orange

⅔ cup (1½ dL) sugar

2 Tb orange or apricot liqueur and 1 Tb Cognac or rum

Place the apricots in a saucepan and soak in vermouth and water several hours or overnight until tender. Then simmer with cinnamon and zest of orange for 10 minutes; add the sugar and simmer 10 minutes more or until very tender. Drain thoroughly and purée, using food processor or vegetable mill. Boil down cooking liquid (if any) to a thick syrup, and stir into the purée along with the liqueur.

🕐 May be completed a week or more in advance; cover and refrigerate.

Confectioners Butter Cream:
For 1 to 1½ cups
Make just before using

8 ounces (225 g) unsalted butter

10 ounces (285 g; 2 cups sifted directly into cup) confectioners sugar

2 egg yolks

1 Tb pure vanilla extract

3 to 4 Tb orange or apricot liqueur, Cognac, or rum

Equipment

An electric mixer

Beat the butter in a bowl over hot water just until softened, then beat in the sugar and continue for a minute or so until light and fluffy. Add the egg yolks, beating for 1 minute, then beat in the vanilla and liqueur. If too soft, beat over cold water until of easy spreading consistency.

Assembling the cake
(and additional ingredients)

About 1 cup (¼ L) confectioners sugar in a sieve or shaker

2 cups (about 8 ounces or 240 g) shaved almonds, lightly toasted

Lightly whipped and sweetened cream to pass with the cake (optional)

Equipment

A serving board or tray to hold the cake; wax paper; a flexible-blade spatula; rubber spatulas

The meringue layers break easily, but don't worry if they do; breaks—or San Andreas faults, as one California friend terms them—can be disguised. Save the best one for the top of the cake, 2 more for layers, and the final one is there just in case. Place double layers of wax paper strips on the serving board in such a way that they can be slipped out from sides and ends of cake after icing.

Set the least attractive of the meringue layers on the board, adjusting the wax paper to fit just under its edges. Reserving almost two-thirds of the butter filling to ice the sides of the cake, spread half of what remains on the meringue layer, then cover with half of the apricot purée. Set a second meringue layer on top, and repeat with a spreading of butter cream and the remaining apricot. Top with a final meringue layer, and if it is unblemished dust with a coating of confectioners sugar. (If it is irreparably cracked, too much so to be disguised with sugar, ice it with butter cream and later sprinkle with almonds.)

Spread butter cream all around the sides of the cake. Then, with the palm of one hand, brush almonds all around to make an informal decoration. (Scatter almonds also on top, if you have the San Andreas fault to deal with.) Chill the cake—you may wish to cover it with a long box.

❶   May be refrigerated for a day or two; the meringue layers gradually soften as the cake sits. Cake may be frozen; thaw in the refrigerator for several hours.

Serving

Cut cake into serving pieces from one of the small ends; a dollop of lightly whipped cream on the side goes nicely with the tart apricot filling.

Remarks:

This recipe allows for a good amount of butter cream, and you may wish to set a little aside. Then, if a reasonable amount of cake is left over, you can refrost the cut end and present, for all the world, a fresh new cake for its next go-around. As an aid to keeping the meringue-nut layers more crisp, you could paint the top of the bottom one, both sides of the middle one, and the bottom of the top layer with the following apricot glaze, letting it set for several minutes before filling the cake.

Apricot Glaze:

Boil up the contents of a 12-ounce (340-g) jar of apricot preserves with 3 tablespoons sugar, stirring, until last drops from a spoon are thick and sticky—and glaze reaches 238°F/115°C. Push through a sieve and use while still warm; return any left over to jar and keep for future glazings.

The fourth meringue layer

If you are sure of your layer stability, you can pulverize this one and either stir it into your apricot purée, or save it for a dessert topping. Or freeze it, and when you want finger cookies, cut it into crosswise strips with a serrated knife, sawing gently; cover with a sifting of confectioners sugar, or the icing of your choice.

❶ *Timing*

This is a relatively fancy meal and involves quite a bit of work, but not much has to be done at the last minute. You can accomplish most of your marketing days in advance. The meringue-nut layers can be baked months beforehand if you freeze them, and the apricots can be cooked a week or more ahead. Just don't forget to thaw your ducks.

You'll need only about five minutes between first and second courses to crisp the duck cracklings and warm the breast slices; and just a moment before the third course to finish the broccoli if you have blanched it in advance.

Not long before announcing dinner, slip the dishes containing legs and skin strips into the oven. They can have sat an hour all prepared, and so can the breasts in their frying pan. You should get your wine bottles ready for evening, chilling your whites, two hours before dinner.

Pre-roast, peel, and carve the ducks, if you're doing them the slow way, in the afternoon.

Early on the day of the party, you can assemble the cake and refrigerate it, purée the parsnips, and blanch the broccoli and the zucchini boats.

Menu Variations

The appetizer: Rather than crab you could serve caviar, or any shellfish: mussels, oysters, clams, scallops, shrimp, lobster. (See "Fish Talk," page 29.)

The main course: The ragout with garlic (bonus recipe) is wonderful, and very easy to serve, but you'd have to change your vegetables accordingly, as the recipe suggests. With the roast, you could omit the zucchini boats and just serve a plain parsnip purée in a dish, but no other way of cooking parsnips would suit roast duck so well. You might substitute a purée of turnips, celery root, or potatoes for the parsnips.

The vegetable course: This is probably the ideal way to cook broccoli. Any sauce but butter and lemon would be too rich on this menu, and a Polonaise garnish of browned crumbs and sieved egg would repeat the crumbs on the duck parts.

The dessert: You could fill your baked layers with puréed dried prunes. Or you could use very stiff, wine-flavored applesauce.

Leftovers

The appetizer: Since the crab is already seasoned, I wouldn't try it in a hot dish, but it would make fine stuffing for hard-boiled eggs or delicious sandwiches.

The main dish: Duck scraps are good in soup, or in a pilaf, or sauced in cocktail puffs or patty shells with drinks. Paul and I like to make a cannibal lunch for ourselves, picking the carcass (which I've roasted 15 to 20 minutes after its bloody carving). Then it goes into the stockpot.

The vegetable course: If you passed the lemon and butter sauce separately, any remaining unseasoned broccoli would be nice in a salad, soup, or timbale.

The dessert: Since I make a rectangular rather than round cake, I save a bit of butter cream, then beat up the butter cream to soften it, refrost the cut end of the cake as described earlier, and serve it again.

Postscript

The keynote of this dinner is flavor, and the duck dominates. If you think about this menu, you'll see that every dish on it was carefully chosen to contrast, in taste and color, with the duck—except the parsnips, which are such a good accompaniment to the bird that the two flavors almost combine in the mouth. Duck deserves this sort of "feature presentation." Having devised a way of dealing with its eccentricities, I serve it much oftener now, as the centerpiece of a luxurious dinner—as well as the grand main course for a plain family dinner. Duck has so much natural flavor and succulence that it is really one of my favorite meat treats.

Post-Postscript: A birthday bonus recipe

The following recipe is totally different in flavor from the roast duck preceding, is very little trouble to do, and is quite good reheated. For a larger birthday party, say 10 to 12 people, I think this would be tidier to serve. I'd buy 3 ducks and increase all the recipe proportions to match. With it I'd serve broccoli flowerettes and baked baby tomatoes, and perhaps a purée of some sort (like the parsnips recipe above, or a purée of turnips or rutabagas, or the potato and turnip purée in *Mastering I),* or, instead of a purée, a mixture of steamed rice sautéed with little mushroom *duxelles,* or plain mashed potatoes. You would never know how much garlic this lovely duck dish contains if the cook didn't tell you. I wouldn't even call this a "garlic sauce"—it's just a satiny, full-flavored nap for the duck meat.

Ragout of Duck with Twenty Cloves of Garlic

For 4 servings

A 4- to 5-pound (2- to 2¼-kg) duckling

1 head garlic, unpeeled, separated into cloves and roughly chopped

2 medium-size ripe tomatoes

1 Tb tomato sauce (if needed for taste and color)

Herbs and spices: 4 whole allspice berries, ½ tsp fennel seeds, ½ tsp thyme, 1 imported bay leaf

½ cup (1 dL) dry white French vermouth

1 cup (¼ L) brown duck stock or beef bouillon

Salt and pepper

Parsley sprigs

Preliminaries

Split the duck down the back on both sides of backbone and reserve backbone for duck stock, along with wing ends, which you sever at the elbows. Cut the peel off the gizzard and add to stock ingredients along with the neck. Cut the duck into 4 pieces, giving more breast

meat to the wing portions than to the leg portions to even things out. Cut off and discard fatty skin pieces and any interior fat. If you wish to do so—and it makes the best sauce—prepare a duck stock by sautéing the backbone, wing, neck, and gizzard peel with ½ cup (1 dL) each chopped onions and carrots; when lightly browned, drain off fat, add water to cover, salt lightly, simmer for an hour, strain, and degrease.

Browning and simmering the duck

Prick the skin of the duck pieces all over at ½-inch (1½-cm) intervals and brown very slowly on all sides in a heavy chicken fryer or casserole, concentrating especially on the skin sides to render out as much fat as possible. Then drain out fat, add the unpeeled garlic cloves, tomatoes and optional tomato sauce, herbs, spices, vermouth, and stock to the pan, and season lightly with salt and pepper. Bring to the simmer, cover, and simmer slowly for about an hour, turning and basting occasionally, until duck leg and wing meat is just tender when pierced with a sharp-pronged fork. Remove from heat and let cool for 10 minutes or so, basting occasionally.

Remove duck pieces from pan, cut off the skin, and cut skin into strips. Sauté the strips slowly in a covered pan until they brown lightly, crisp, and render their fat; drain on paper towels and reserve. Meanwhile, thoroughly degrease the cooking liquid and strain it, pushing the garlic against the sieve to purée it into the liquid; boil down rapidly until sauce is lightly thickened. Return duck pieces to sauce and heat briefly, basting, to warm them. Carefully correct seasoning of sauce, and the duck is ready to serve.

🕐 May be done somewhat in advance, if you keep the duck pieces barely warm in their sauce, and reheat to the simmer just before serving.

Serving

Arrange duck on a platter and spoon the sauce over it. Decorate with parsley sprigs and sprinkle cracklings over the duck (you may wish to include the duck's liver, sautéed as the cracklings cook).

*Don't try to fool a dieter's appetite. Excite it.
Beautiful, contrasting, full-flavored, this is
food, not fodder; and a little feels like a lot.*

Lo-Cal Banquet

Menu
For 6 people

Angosoda Cocktail

❧

*Appetizer of Shrimp, Green Beans, and
Sliced Mushrooms*

❧

*Chicken Bouillabaisse with Rouille,
a Garlic and Pimiento Sauce*

❧

Steamed Rice

❧

Caramel-crowned Steam-baked Apples

❧

*Suggested wines:
A hearty Pinot Blanc or
white Châteauneuf-du-Pape*

When you're on a diet, do you feel you "just can't give a dinner party"? Or does it depress you to plan a menu for dieting guests? I sympathize, because "diet food," as such, is dismal food: no fun to plan, no fun to fix. Pure labor in vain. Fake food—I mean those patented substances chemically flavored and mechanically bulked out to kill the appetite and deceive the gut—is unnatural, almost immoral, a bane to good eating and good cooking. I'd rather look at it this way: nothing, except conscious virtue, can mitigate the groaning intervals between a dieter's meals; but why should the meals, too, be a penance? On the contrary. Light food for sharp appetites should stimulate, then satisfy, with calories allotted to bulk and balance and a few strategically disposed—like crack troops—where they'll be most telling: for flavoring, for unctuous or crackling texture, for mouth-filling opulence. The relish of it! Dieters are the best audience a cook ever has, for they savor and remember every morsel.

Of course Paul and I have to diet every now and then. It helps to have happy, busy lives and to get some exercise. Believing in the healthy body's wisdom, that what you want is what you need, we seek variety and practice moderation, eat less and enjoy it more than when we were young string beans. But sometimes we have absentminded or greedy spells, and the day comes when we start planning and get out the old notebook. All right: 1200 calories each per diem. Breakfast, 150; lunch, 200; dinner, 800. Fifty calories are left out, you'll notice; it's our error factor—a small one, since we are faithful about recording every stray bite or sample while cooking. Authorities vary in the calorie amounts they give, so we take the highest we can find for each item. Better, we think, to deprive than to deceive ourselves; but we soften the deprivation by allotting 100 of our dinner calories to a glass of good wine. It never tastes better!

At parties, we eat a bit of everything, but we are glad of the growing fashion for lighter, more savory menus. More thoughtful planning, more scrupulous preparation are the modern cook's response to the challenge: make every calorie count. Don't hesitate to invite nondieters to the meal I'm about to describe, or even the lean and hungry young. You can double quantities, add bread or extras like cookies or cakes for dessert for them, or otherwise supplement or vary the menu (see Menu Variations); but it's certainly not necessary. This meal is so delicious, they'll take big helpings and return for seconds; but a moderate portion of each dish, though you'd hardly believe it, adds up to a sensible 678 calories. There's no trick to it, and no secret—only a well-considered application of the simplest principles of sound gastronomy: contrast, balance, beauty, savor, and style.

A subtle appetizer of shrimp, fresh green beans, and thinly sliced raw mushrooms arranged on watercress; a bouillabaisse of chicken, robust and aromatic, heaped on steamed rice and richly enhanced with a Provençal *rouille;* and a fresh, fragrant dessert of apples, steam-baked with wine, lemon, and stick cinnamon, then webbed with glistening caramel—this meal has everything. Everything plus. The ingredients aren't expensive; most of the work can be done in advance; and, since the dishes are all cooked on top of the stove, you won't waste fuel. And finally, the leftovers: delicious, elegant, and infinitely transformable. Sometimes I buy and cook the whole works in double quantities. Why not have two meals for the effort of one?

A Note on Alcohol and Calories:

As opposed to wine, which is a food as well as something to lift your spirits, liquor is full of empty but horribly real calories that don't nourish you. Only the most serious dieters need omit wine altogether, but instead of a cocktail I suggest you try

The Angosoda Cocktail:

In a large, handsome stemmed glass, place several cubes of ice, dash on a few drops of Angostura Bitters, add a slice of lime, and fill up with sparkling water. The fizz, the rosy color, and the dot of green are attractive, and it tastes like a real drink.

On Wine in Cooking:

Calorie counters can use a lot, and I do. The alcohol, which carries the calories, evaporates away in a moment of cooking. The flavor, now a bit softer and subtler, remains to give your dish complexity and depth of taste that make it more satisfying as well as more delicious.

Preparations

Marketing and Storage:
Staples to have on hand

Olive oil
Salt
Peppercorns
Granulated sugar
Pure vanilla extract
Maraschino cherries
Hot pepper sauce
Whole fennel seeds
Dried thyme, dill, and bay leaves
Dried oregano (if you can't get fresh basil) ▼
Saffron threads ▼
Stick cinnamon
Dried orange peel ▼
Angostura Bitters
Plain canned tomato sauce
Long-grain untreated white Carolina rice ▼
Onions and shallots or scallions
Garlic
Fresh bread crumbs (in the freezer;
     see page 5)
Lemons (1) and limes
Eggs (1)
Canned pimiento
Dry white wine or dry white French vermouth
Soda water

Specific ingredients for this menu

Shrimp (24 "large medium") ▼
Chicken (two fryers, or 16 pieces of cut-up
     chicken) ▼
Green beans (½ pound or 225 g)
Mushrooms (12)
Watercress
Parsley
Leeks (about 4)
Tomatoes (about 12)▼
Apples (6, Golden Delicious if possible) ▼

▶ *Remarks:*
Staples

Dried oregano: substituted for dried basil, because I don't think the latter has much flavor. *Fresh basil:* grow your own if you have a sunny spot; it's incomparable. *Saffron threads:* specified because powdered saffron may not be pure. The real saffron threads, which bear the pollen in a certain kind of crocus, are something of a luxury, but you use them sparingly. And you must, because too much saffron produces a medicinal taste which can't be corrected. *Dried orange peel:* to make your own, using a vegetable peeler take 2-inch-long (5-cm) strips of zest off an orange, let dry for a day or two on paper towels, then bottle—keeps indefinitely. *Long-grain untreated white Caro-*

lina rice is best for steaming. The plump, nutty-flavored grains of Italian rice will too often degenerate into a gluey mass.

Ingredients for this menu

Shrimp: if you're lucky enough to live near the seacoast and to have a trustworthy market, you may be able to get them fresh and alive. Otherwise, your safest bet is to buy them raw in the shell, frozen solid in a block. Keep them that way until ready to cook; then thaw rapidly in lots of cold water and peel as soon as you can detach them from the frozen mass. Devein them: if you see a black line, it's the intestinal vein; you can usually pull it out from the large end without slitting the shrimp. (See "Fish Talk," page 29, for illustration.) *Chicken:* fryers are perfect for the fricassee method, which you employ in making this bouilla-baisse. It is easy to cut up your own.

But if you decide on ready-cut chicken, note that thighs are the best buy: they are cheaper than drumsticks and have more flesh and less bone. Before storing or cooking chicken, be on the safe side: rinse with warm water, inside and out, and dry before refrigerating. If you're going to keep it more than a day or two, refrigerate it in a plastic bag set in a bowl of ice cubes which you renew as needed. *Vegetables:* refrigerate unwashed beans in a plastic bag until ready to prepare; mushrooms and leeks ditto. Parsley and cress can be freshened by soaking several hours in cold water. Then drain; shake dry and roll up loosely in paper towels and refrigerate in plastic bags. Be sure your garlic is not dried out. Sniff your bottled herbs and spices for freshness—they should always be kept out of the light. *Tomatoes:* be sure you get in your tomatoes several days in advance to let them ripen properly. *Apples:* some of the most savory varieties turn into mush when steamed. Depending on where you live, try Golden Delicious, Rome Beauty, York Imperial, Greening, Newton, Monroe, or Northern Spy. The Golden Delicious, available in most regions, is always reliable, and its flavor will be enhanced by the spice and wine; its green-yellow skin is a nice pale topaz after cooking.

Appetizer of Shrimp, Green Beans, and Sliced Mushrooms

For 6 people

½ pound (225 g) green beans
12 large mushrooms
Fresh lemon juice
24 "large medium" shrimp
¾ cup (1 ¾ dL) dry white French vermouth or 1 cup (¼ L) dry white wine
1 Tb minced shallots or scallions
½ tsp salt
¼ tsp dried dill weed
Several grinds black pepper
Watercress or parsley
Garnish: lemon wedges; small pitcher olive oil

The beans

Several hours or the morning before serving, wash the fresh green beans. Snap off each end with your fingers, pulling down the bean's

seam to remove any lurking string. Plunge the beans into 3 to 4 quarts or liters of rapidly boiling salted water and boil uncovered 5 to 8 minutes (tasting frequently after 5 minutes) until beans are just cooked through. They are done when still a little crunchy and still bright green. (There has been a vogue for describing such beans as "crunchily underdone," but I do think such terms are used by those who have been brought up on frozen beans, which have no crunch, and little taste either, for that matter. Properly cooked beans are just cooked through; improperly cooked beans are either over- or underdone.) Once the beans are just cooked through, then, drain in a colander, run cold water into the kettle, and dump the beans back in to refresh them and stop the cooking—this also serves to retain their fresh texture and bright-green color. Drain again, dry in a towel, and chill in a plastic bag.

The mushrooms

An hour before serving, trim the fresh large fine mushrooms, wash rapidly, and dry. Slice thinly and neatly, and toss in a little fresh lemon juice to prevent discoloration. Arrange on a dish, cover with plastic wrap, and chill.

The shrimp

Several hours or the morning before serving, simmer the raw peeled shrimp in the dry white French vermouth or dry white wine, minced shallots or scallions, salt, dried dill weed, and pepper. Toss and turn the shrimp in the liquid for 2 to 3 minutes, until shrimp curl and just become springy to the touch. Remove shrimp to a bowl, then rapidly boil down the cooking liquid to a syrupy consistency; pour it back over the shrimp, tossing several times. Chill.

To serve

An hour before serving, slice the shrimp in half horizontally—so they will look like more shrimp!—and arrange tastefully, either on individual plates or on a platter, with watercress or parsley, the beans, and the mushrooms. Cover with plastic wrap and chill until dinner time. Pass lemon wedges with the appetizer and a little pitcher of good olive oil for those who are permitted such luxury.

Chicken Bouillabaisse with Rouille

Fricassee of chicken with leeks, tomatoes, herbs, and wine, with a garlic and pimiento sauce on the side

For 6 people with ample leftovers

Two 3½-pound (1¼-kg) fryers, or 16 chicken pieces, such as thighs, drumsticks, breast halves
⅓ cup (¾ dL) olive oil
3 cups (¾ L) combination of thinly sliced white of leek and onions, or onions only
3 to 4 large cloves garlic
4 cups (1 L) fresh tomato pulp (about 2½ pounds or 1 kg tomatoes, peeled, seeded, juiced, sliced)
2 to 4 Tb plain tomato sauce, or as needed, for added flavor
½ tsp fennel seeds, 1 tsp thyme, large pinch saffron threads, two 2-inch (5-cm) strips dried orange peel, 2 imported bay leaves
Salt
2 cups (½ L) dry white French vermouth
Pepper
Fresh chopped parsley

Preliminary cooking of the chicken

If you are cutting up the chicken yourself, as I like to do, see illustrated directions in *J.C.'s Kitchen*, page 228. Dry the chicken pieces and place with the olive oil in a large skillet or casserole over moderate heat. Simmer about 10 minutes, turning the pieces several times in the hot oil until they stiffen slightly but do not brown. While the chicken is cooking, wash and slice the leeks, peel and slice the onion, and peel and chop the garlic.

When chicken has stiffened, remove it to a side dish, leaving oil in pan. Stir in the leeks, onions, and garlic; cook slowly 5 minutes or so, until fairly soft but not browned. Meanwhile, peel, seed, and juice the tomatoes; slice them roughly and fold into the leeks, onions, and garlic along with the fennel, thyme, saffron, orange peel, and bay leaves. Taste, and if the tomatoes aren't flavorful enough, add a little tomato sauce as needed. Then salt the chicken on all sides. Arrange in the pan, basting with the vegetables. Cover and cook 5 minutes; turn, baste, cover, and cook 5 minutes more.

🕐   Recipe may be completed to this point several hours or even a day in advance. Let cool, then cover and refrigerate. Bring to the simmer again, covered, before proceeding.

Finishing the cooking

An hour before serving, pour in the wine, cover the pan, and simmer 15 to 20 minutes more, basting and turning the chicken several times just until the pieces are tender when pierced with a fork. Remove chicken to a side dish, tilt pan, and skim off all visible cooking fat; then rapidly boil down cooking liquid to thicken it. Taste very carefully for seasoning, adding salt and pepper to taste. Return chicken to pan, baste with the sauce, set cover askew, and keep warm (but well below the simmer) until serving time. When ready to bring to the table, arrange the chicken and sauce on a hot platter and decorate with parsley. Pass the special sauce (next recipe) separately.

Dieting Notes:

To cut down on calories, you can peel the skin off the chicken after it is cooked as described in the preceding paragraph and do a very thorough degreasing of the sauce before boiling it down—even pour it through a sieve, so that you can remove the fat more easily from the liquid. Then return contents of sieve and skimmed liquid to the cooking pan with the chicken.

Rouille

Garlic and pimiento sauce. To serve with a bouillabaisse, or with pasta, boiled potatoes or beans, boiled fish or chicken, and so forth

6 cloves garlic

1 tsp salt

12 large leaves fresh basil (or 1 tsp dried oregano)

⅓ cup (¾ dL) canned red pimiento

⅓ cup (¾ dL) lightly pressed down fresh white nonsweet bread crumbs

1 egg yolk

1 cup (¼ L) olive oil

Freshly ground pepper

Drops of hot pepper sauce

Equipment

A mortar and pestle are nice, but you can use the bottom of a ladle and a sturdy bowl, which, if not metal, should be set on a mat so it won't crack.

Purée the garlic cloves through a press into a mortar or bowl. Then pound the garlic with the salt into a smooth paste. Pound in the basil or oregano. When the mixture is smooth, add the pimiento and pound again; then add the crumbs, and finally pound in the egg yolk. Switch from pestle to wire whisk and, drop by drop at first, beat in the olive oil until mixture has thickened like mayonnaise, then beat in the oil a little faster to make a quite stiff sauce. Season highly with pepper and hot sauce.

⏱ May be made a day or two in advance. Refrigerate in a covered container; remove and let come to room temperature an hour before serving.

Remarks:
This redolent sauce, named for its rich rust color, is high in calories; but even a small dollop adds a voluptuous texture and hearty flavor to a serving of the bouillabaisse. I find it more satisfying to take one piece of chicken, rather than two, and enjoy it with the *rouille*.

Steamed Rice

For 4½ cups

1½ cups (3½ dL) plain raw white rice
2 tsp salt

In a large pot, bring 6 to 8 cups (1½ to 2 L) water to rolling boil, add rice and salt, and boil 7 to 8 minutes, or until *al dente*. Test by biting a grain. It should have a tiny hard core. Drain in a colander, and rinse under cold running water to remove all traces of starch—which would make the rice gummy.

🕐   Rice may be cooked ahead to this point even a day in advance, and its final cooking finished later.

About 15 minutes before serving, set colander of rice over a kettle of boiling water (bottom of colander should not rest in the water). Cover colander with a lid or a clean towel and steam just until rice is tender. Toss it once or twice to be sure it is steaming evenly. Do not overcook: ends of rice should remain rounded (splayed-out ends declare rice to be overdone).

Caramel-crowned Steam-baked Apples

1 cup (2 dL) white wine, or half wine or dry white vermouth and water, or water only
2 tsp pure vanilla extract
½ lemon
6 cooking apples (Golden Delicious or others that will keep their shape)
4 or more Tb sugar
Maraschino cherries
½ cup (1 dL) sugar
3 Tb water
Stick cinnamon
Equipment

Get a steaming rack, now available almost anywhere. It's perfect for most fruits and vegetables, though not for rice. The kind I like doesn't work for pudding, either, since it is lifted out of the pot by a vertical center handle. It's made of stainless steel and consists of a round perforated bottom dish standing on folding legs an inch or so high. Hinged around the circumference of the disk is a series of perforated flaps that fold inward for storage and outward, against the edge of the saucepan, when the steamer is in use.

Into a saucepan large enough to hold steamer and apples comfortably with a cover, put the liquid, vanilla, cinnamon, and several strips of

lemon peel, adding water if necessary so you have ½ inch (1½ cm) liquid in the pan for the steaming operation. Wash and core the apples, and peel half the way down from blossom (small) end, dropping peel into saucepan with steaming liquid—to give added flavor and body to it for later. Place steamer in pan and the apples, peeled ends up, upon it. Squeeze the juice of the half lemon over the apples, and sprinkle on as much sugar as you think appropriate for the apples you are using. Bring to the simmer, cover the pan closely, and regulate heat so that liquid is barely simmering—too intense a steam will cause the apples to disintegrate—and keep checking on their progress. They should be done in 15 to 20 minutes, when you can pierce them easily with a small knife.

🕐 Apples may be cooked a day or more ahead and served cold.

Set the apples on a serving dish or on individual plates or bowls. Remove steamer from pan; boil down the cooking liquid rapidly until lightly syrupy, sweeten to taste, and strain over the apples. Decorate each with a maraschino cherry.

The caramel
Shortly before serving, prepare a caramel syrup. Bring ½ cup (1 dL) sugar and 3 table-spoons water to the boil in a small, heavy saucepan, then remove from heat and swirl pan until all sugar has dissolved and liquid is clear—an essential step in sugar-boiling operations, to prevent sugar from crystallizing. Then return to heat, bring again to the boil, cover, and boil rapidly for a minute or so until bubbles are large and thick, indicating that liquid has almost evaporated. Remove cover and boil, swirling pan gently by its handle but *never never* stirring, until syrup turns a nice, not-too-dark caramel brown. Immediately set bottom of pan in cold water and stir with a spoon for a few seconds until caramel cools slightly and begins to thicken. It should ooze off the spoon in lazy, thick strands. This is important, because if you put it on the apples too soon, when it's too hot or too thin, it'll just slide off onto the dish. Rapidly decorate the apples with strands of syrup dripped over them from tip of spoon, waving it over them in a circular spiral to make attractive patterns.

Remarks:
To clean the caramel pan and the spoon easily, simply fill pan with water and set to simmer for a few minutes to dissolve all traces of caramel.

◑ *Timing*

This is an easy menu, and you can be leisurely getting most of it done ahead. If you want to do as much as possible in advance, start by deciding to serve the apples cold. Then look at the recipes for suggestions and for the points marked ◑ . For this menu, you can start as much as two days ahead of time.

There's only one last-minute job: as your guests sit down to their appetizer, turn on the heat under the rice for its final steaming.

Half an hour before serving the main course, finish simmering the chicken.

An hour before your guests arrive, take the *rouille* from the refrigerator, but don't give it a final stir until it has reached room temperature. Slice limes for your Angosoda Cocktail, and place in a covered dish.

About two hours before the party, arrange the appetizer on a large platter or individual plates, cover with plastic wrap, and refrigerate. Chill white wine if you're serving it.

Several hours—but not the day—before, accomplish the second stage of the bouillabaisse, that of boiling down the sauce, tasting and correcting the seasoning. Wash, blanch, drain, and dry green beans. Clean and slice mushrooms, toss in lemon juice to keep white, and chill. Prepare and chill shrimp. Make a caramel sauce, let cool a bit, and decorate the apples.

Still on the day of your party, start cooking chicken.

A day or so before, you can steam the apples and start the rice.

The bouilla-"base," the concentrate of vegetables, herbs, and wine, though better flavored if made with the chicken in it, can in fact be made well in advance. It doesn't hurt to cook the vegetables the day before you make the "base." Keep them covered and chilled.

The *rouille* actually tastes better if you make it a day before serving and let its flavors marry in the refrigerator.

Menu Variations

The *appetizer* could be varied by substituting asparagus tips for the beans, or fine small spinach leaves for the cress, or almost any shellfish for the shrimp. Raw bay or sea scallops may be marinated in fresh lime juice and seasonings, which delicately cook them. Green beans and mushrooms on cress, without shellfish, are delicious, perhaps with cherry tomatoes and a scattering of finely chopped chives or scallions.

The *bouillabaisse,* as you know, is most familiar as a hearty soup containing a mixture of fish. In this more condensed form, which of course you eat with a fork, you could exchange chicken for a firm-fleshed fish, for scallops, or for salt cod (but allow time to freshen it). It makes a grand main dish for vegetarians if you use chunks of presalted, sautéed eggplant instead of chicken; or else one of the bulkier pastas, like *rotini* and *rigatoni.* Only steamed rice is a proper complement to the bouillabaisse, so I have no alternative to suggest.

The *dessert* can be made with pears instead of apples. It can be lightened by omitting the caramel, or enriched by passing, separately, a bowl of custard sauce or lightly whipped cream.

*Rigatoni (left) and *rotini**

Leftovers

Rice: if you have extra, make a cold rice salad, or serve it in a soup, or use it to thicken a sauce *soubise.* As for the *bouillabaisse,* you can reheat it, and it will still be delicious. But I love it cold as a luncheon dish. If I plan on that, I usually pull the skin off all the chicken pieces (don't like cold chicken skin!), then arrange the chicken in a nice serving dish and spoon the sauce over. After chilling, the sauce jells; before serving, I remove any surface fat and sprinkle a bit of fresh chopped parsley over all. Delicious just as it is, or arranged on a bed of lettuce and decorated with black olives. The rice could even accompany the chicken again as a cold salad.

Here's another idea I developed after the television show, when I had quantities of chicken in bouillabaisse to play with. After reheating batches of it twice, serving it cold once, and still having more, I decided to purée the sauce in a food processor. It turned into a kind of horrid pudding, so I simmered it with a cup of chicken broth and tried to strain it, with no success. Then I thought of my trusty potato ricer. I lined it with a double thickness of washed cheesecloth, filled it with a ladleful of my rosy pudding, gave it a squeeze, and out came a savory, translucent, satiny rose liquid which I spooned over my chilled and peeled chicken and chilled again. A happy discovery.

The rouille will keep for a week or more and is delicious as a spaghetti sauce, with boiled or broiled fish or chicken, with boiled or baked potatoes, or stirred into a minestrone-type soup.

The apples are excellent cold, and will keep several days refrigerated in a covered dish. Or you may slice the flesh and serve with a fruit sauce (frozen raspberries, thawed, puréed, and strained, are good, though rather high in sugar). To make more juice, simmer a fresh apple with a cinnamon stick, a slice of lemon, and an ounce or so of vermouth, then strain.

Postscript

Here's your calorie count. I put it last so as not to deter nondieters from trying this excellent meal—for the bald numbers are so shockingly low you may not believe, before tasting, that I have been talking about real food all this time.

Salad of shrimp, green beans, and sliced mushrooms	66
Chicken bouillabaisse (2 sauced pieces)	250
Rouille (1 tablespoon)	75
Steamed rice (½ cup)	100
1 apple with syrup and caramel crown	187

The ingredients
(calories per 3½ oz or 100 g):

Raw shrimp		91
Cooked green beans		25
Raw mushrooms		28
Watercress		19
Fryer, light meat with skin, without	120,	101
dark meat with skin, without	132,	112
Olive oil		884
Leeks		52
Onions		38
Raw tomatoes		22
Tomato sauce		39
Bread crumbs		392
Egg yolk		348
Cooked rice		109
Raw apple		117
Sugar		385
Wine, dry, sweet	85,	137
Gin, rum, vodka, whiskey (80 proof)		231
Beer		42

The calorie counts are those given in an excellent handbook by Bernice K. Watt and Annabel L. Merrill, *Composition of Foods: Raw, Processed, Prepared* (Agriculture Handbook No. 8, U.S. Department of Agriculture, Washington, D.C., revised December 1963).

Essay

An assortment of New England fish and shellfish

Fish Talk

The average American consumes only eleven pounds of fish a year, which argues that he doesn't like it much…"it" meaning not the whole marvelous universe of fish, but the frozen packaged fillets which are his staple purchase. Habit, I think, is why many of us buy fish that way, habit and caution. Freezing *seems* a safeguard when everybody knows that fish deteriorates from the moment it leaves the sea (unlike meat, which has to be hung for an interval to become tender). And it's true that a good fish which is gutted, filleted, and flash-frozen (in immaculate conditions, and as soon as caught) and which arrives on your stove in no more than three months—having been maintained throughout that time at a temperature of $-5°F/-20.5°C$—is very fine eating indeed. You will not often find such fish, and only rarely from mass packagers: remember, the majority of them get most of their fish from abroad and cannot control shipboard conditions. I think it's safer to find a dealer you can trust, a specialist in fish who knows his suppliers.

Anyway, if you do buy frozen packaged fillets (and I'd certainly rather have them than no fish at all), open the package in the store and inspect it with a jaundiced eye and alert nostrils. Complain to the manager (who will pass it on and maybe improve his stock) *if:* the cut edges look dry; or the flesh has whitish patches; or there is any discoloration, especially a yellowish or even rusty streak down the center of the fillet's darker side. The same goes for frozen fillets bought by the piece. Frozen whole fish should be completely encased in a glaze of ice, and shrimp should be frozen in their shells in a solid block. Thawed fish should be treated like fresh: bedded on ice in the dealer's case.

If you buy any thawed or fresh fish, remember that fish has no odor when just caught; in the store it should have at most a mild, faint, fresh scent, which I find very appetizing. Insist on the sniff test; and check the thermometer in the freezer compartment: $1°F$, no higher—and preferably lower.

Away from the coast, you really can't expect to find the very perishable shellfish, like shrimp and scallops, sold fresh; twenty years ago, any fresh seafood—and all but local freshwater fish, like the beautiful Idaho trout and upper Great.Lakes whitefish—was hard to find anywhere inland. But nowadays, with our air-freight network so well developed, with the Bureau of Fisheries' careful policing, and with modern techniques of aquaculture, we could, if we insisted on it, have fresh-caught fish available daily all over the country, at least in cities and towns. Once one has tasted it, little else will do; it's like a sunny day compared to a smoggy one.

It is not difficult to identify fresh-caught fish. The skin color is intense and bright, the gills are bright red inside, the eyes are bright and bulging. After two days, the eyes begin to flatten; don't buy a fish whose eyes are flush with its skin. Another test, especially if you are buying fresh fish by the piece, is to press the flesh with a fingertip; the imprint should quickly disappear. You can soon become expert; but you still need a good dealer. The Japanese Americans, who use only the most

perfect fish in raw dishes like sushi and sashimi, are the people to follow. If you are lucky, like me, in having a local Japanese-American population, find out where they buy fish.

Fresh fish will stay fresh longest when it is kept at a temperature of 30.5°F/−1°C, which you achieve by packing in ice. Incidentally, fish does not freeze at this temperature— water does. The best way to keep fish when you get home is to unwrap it, place it in a plastic bag, and set it in the refrigerator in a bowl of ice sprinkled with a little coarse salt; pour off the water as it accumulates and renew the ice twice a day. Very fresh fish will keep even two or three days when handled this way.

Shellfish must be alive until eaten or cooked. When you buy bivalves (oysters, clams, mussels, scallops, etc.), they should be tightly closed. If the shells are slightly ajar, rap them sharply; they should close at once. If any bivalve feels unduly light, it means the occupant is dead. If unduly heavy (especially in the case of clams or mussels), the shell may be full of seabed sand or mud. Don't use any with chipped or broken shells.

The general rule for storing bivalves is to take them home promptly, scrub the shells thoroughly with a stiff brush, and refrigerate.

Cover oysters with dampened paper towels and foil, and be sure to store them with the larger, more convex side down so the oyster may bathe, and live, in its juices.

Now that the sturgeon are returning to a few of our refreshed rivers, it may not be long before we're all preparing a cheap and nutritious household staple: our own caviar. Meanwhile, since we have relearned the 2000-year-old art of oyster culture, oyster prices are on the decline. Where I live, a dozen great succulent Cotuits, so fresh they twitch under a squirt of lemon juice, cost less than a good delicatessen sandwich. I hope they (or another good variety) are available where you live; and there's no reason they shouldn't be. Refrigerated properly, they keep an amazing four weeks after harvesting; certainly you are safe in storing them at least a week after buying

them. In the 1880s, my own grandmother in rural Illinois would have oysters shipped from the East during the winter months and always kept a barrel of them in her cellar.

Always open oysters *as*, not before, you eat them; savor the flesh and every drop of the liquor, and you will have tasted the very essence of the living, fertile sea. In our family we eat them with spoons rather than the conventional forks, and drink the liquor from the shell.

Except—perhaps—at breakfast (a fine time for them), oysters are best accompanied by quartered lemons, a pepper grinder, buttered dark bread, and a dry white wine. They aren't that hard to open—after all, some Stone Age peoples managed—but since, unlike those of the other bivalves, oysters' shells seal tightly shut and, moreover, overlap, it's difficult to find the seal itself. Oysters can be obdurate, and I am afraid many of us give up and buy them already shucked by a professional. His method is to use a strong, long-bladed knife, both for levering the shells apart and for scraping the inside of each shell in order to detach the firm adductor muscle which binds shell to flesh. I've learned something new since I described this method in detail (in *J.C.'s Kit-*

chen). The oyster's hinge is not as strong as its muscle, and you can lever the shells apart by using an ordinary beer can opener: place the oyster curved side down, hinge toward you; poke around the hinge for an opening into which you can plunge the point of the opener—its curved side down—thrust it in, pry open the hinge, and you'll hear it pop. Once the shells part slightly, use an oyster knife, or even a paring knife, to sever the muscle under the top shell, northeast-by-east side. Protect the oyster-holding hand with a pot holder, and don't jab or shove.

For the occasional diehard, try the conventional method of opening at the side, using an oyster knife. If that doesn't work, the fol-

lowing two methods are inelegant but sure-fire. You can "bill" oysters by knocking off a bit of the lip with a hammer, producing a crevice for your knife tip. Or you can heat them quickly in a 450°F/230°C oven or over a burner, just till the shells part. The flesh will still be cold.

Other bivalves aren't so firmly sealed, which makes them easier to open and harder to keep. Unlike oysters, they should be stored uncovered in circulating air; and, if you ice them, be sure to pour off the melt frequently. The illustration below shows a clam-opening procedure.

To open scallops, the easiest of the lot, just feel with your knife for a vulnerable spot in the seam between the shells, starting about one-third of the way outward from the hinge, and simply lever open. Actually, it's most unlikely you'll be able to buy scallops in their beautiful fluted shells (since these take too much room in the scallop boats' holds). But if you do get some, don't throw away the delicious red or golden tongue-shaped roe, which constitutes one-third of the scallop. Eat it raw or in a *seviche,* or cooked—just as you would the white portion, which is the scallop's muscle and the only part you can usually buy in fish stores. And when you buy them, keep them iced and eat them soon; they don't keep longer than a day or so.

Crustaceans are arthropods, meaning creatures with jointed feet: shrimp, lobsters, various kinds of crab, and crayfish. The best way to buy shrimp, since only one percent of the catch is sold fresh, is frozen: in their shells, in a solid block. (See Remarks in "Lo-Cal Banquet," page 20, for details.) Incidentally, when you see the word "scampi" on a restaurant menu, it undoubtedly means shrimp, since *scampi* is Italian for the rare "Dublin Bay" prawns or langoustine, small lobsterlike sea creatures.

The best-known crabs of the Atlantic are the blue crabs, which when molting are known as soft-shell crabs and are cooked and eaten almost whole; when their shells are hard, you boil them, as you do all other kinds of crab. Unless you live in Alaska, you are not likely to acquire a king crab fresh, and if you did, you might find it an alarming guest: one enormous leg can make a couple of servings. Generally,

These are Eastern bay scallops; the female has an orange roe, the male a gray roe. The fluted shell belongs to the European scallop. (Below) Pulling out the black intestinal vein from a shrimp.

To open clams, insert knife one-third of the way down from the hinge; press, using the fingers of your other hand for leverage; and pry open.

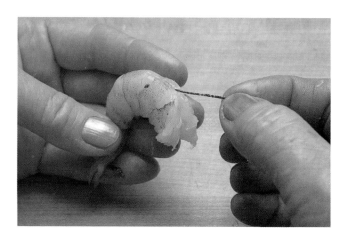

king crabs are sold boiled and frozen in the shell, in segments. Two other well-known varieties are the large delicious Dungeness crab of the Pacific and the stone crab of Florida.

The thing to remember about frozen crabmeat, which is what most of us buy—or really about any frozen flesh—is to thaw it slowly, in the refrigerator, so that lingering ice crystals don't pierce the thawing flesh, making it mushy. An excellent alternative to frozen crabmeat is canned pasteurized crab, which will keep for months in the refrigerator.

There's not space here—or anywhere!—to say all I want to about fish and shellfish: their thousands of fascinating species, their variety of life cycles, their value and their vulnerability, their beauty and their excellence. Though overfishing, careless fishing, and pollution have badly depleted our supply, we can take heart—provided we and our elected representatives remain vigilant. New regulations and treaties, and new techniques of water management and of sea farming (as well as

pond and river farming) are gradually changing all that. Thank goodness, for fish is a good source of protein and trace minerals, has about one-quarter the calories of meat, is more easily digested, cooks many times faster (saving energy), and uses Earth's resources better. An acre of sea can produce 23 tons of oyster meat, for example—150 times the weight of beef produced by an acre of pasture.

The best specific information you can get, and the most up to date (for their research is unending), is from the U.S. Bureau of Fisheries. Its devoted, diligent, and cooperative public servants will share their expertise and enthusiasm with you for the price of a telephone call. For the moment I have to content myself with summarizing my advice in four maxims whose initials—with a wrench or two—spell FISH. Buy fish and shellfish *fresh* whenever you can; buy from an *immaculately* clean place; *store* it on ice; and eat it in a *hurry*.

These lovely crabs are (clockwise from left) the Alaskan king crab, stone crab claws, Dungeness, blue crabs (female with roe), and soft-shell crabs.

A gorgeous spread for people you really want to see; and a revolutionary method to make puff pastry an everyday staple.

Cocktail Party

Menu

Ham Pithiviers, a puff pastry tart

❦

Puffed Cheese Appetizers

❦

Gravlaks, dilled fresh salmon

❦

Minimeatballs

❦

Peking Wings

❦

Oysters and Clams

❦

Stuffed Eggs

❦

Buttered Radishes

❦

Suggested wines:
Red and white wine, your usual bar setup,
and a special cocktail: A la Recherche
de l'Orange Perdue

Cocktail parties aren't what they used to be, and that's all right with me. Goodbye to boozing and starving and crowding and screaming, to five-to-seven and six-to-eight, to the sudden exodus, to the ruined parlor; and goodbye, above all, to that day-after-Christmas feeling, when you realize you never had a minute with the people you most wanted to see. And welcome, with three loud cheers, to easy evenings of good wine and good food and good friends.

We like to give our guests a *spread.* I hate it when people get hungry after a couple of drinks and charge out somewhere to supper before I even get to see them. So Paul and I set out plates and forks and napkins as a hint to stay; and I serve a great big puffy something I baked specially, and something fishy and fresh, and lots of good hearty treats on the side: chicken wings and oysters and clams and stuffed eggs, and meatballs and rabbit food. And peanuts too. Of course we serve the usual drinks—including at least one of Paul's special inventions—but our friends mostly prefer wine for a long evening, so we have plenty of that.

In line with the good new custom of more cheer for fewer people, we give our parties in the kitchen, right in the heart of the house. People can't come into a kitchen and not relax. And we've gotten bored anyway with "Queen Anne in front and Mary Anne behind": the parlor gussied up with coasters and teeny napkins while frenzy reigns out back. Yes, there's some mess. Puff pastry means crumbs and shellfish mean shells. We just line a couple of wastebins with plastic bags which we replace as they fill up and hoist out the back door.

Paul had the thought of making a big wood frame lined with heavy plastic (with a drain for drips) for the cold things. We heap it with ice and set it right on the stove top, where it looks bounteous. We flank it with hot dishes on an electric tray, and use cutting boards to serve a couple of ham Pithiviers tarts, high as hassocks and light as clouds. They're not much work, if you make your puff pastry in advance and do it the fast new way. Puff pastry can be your best friend too, and if you've not yet mastered it, bear in mind three great truths. Don't be afraid of it. Keep it cold. And finally, don't fight it: rest it often, just as you would a fussy baby.

That big slab of fish on the ice mound is *gravlaks,* salmon rubbed with salt, bedded on dill (and spruce twigs if you have them), anointed with Cognac, weighted down, and macerated in the refrigerator for three or four days at least. It's an exquisite preparation, fresher and more delicate than smoked salmon but not raw-tasting (for the salt "cooks" it). I first sampled *gravlaks* in Oslo when Paul was Cultural Attaché at the American Embassy. The salmon was served with scrambled eggs and creamed potatoes as a main course. Delicious! But I also like it for cocktails served with buttered pumpernickel.

Spicy things are nice with cocktails, too, and I always like something hot, so we make minimeatballs of ground beef mixed with a bit of pork sausage for richness, as well as a delightful, vaguely Oriental preparation of chicken wings. Radish roses with little top-knots of sweet butter, stuffed eggs flavored with lemon and anchovy and topped with enormous capers the size of fat peas, and peanuts, of course. Without peanuts, it isn't a cocktail party.

Preparations

Recommended Equipment:
You'll want plenty of beer can openers, oyster knives, and paring knives for the shellfish, and something you can make a bed of ice in: a giant bowl, a washtub, or a deep tray. Or, if you have two sinks, use one for the purpose, as we do our vegetable sink.

A proper rolling pin is essential for puff pastry, one at least 16 inches (40 cm) long. If yours is too short, you're better off with a broomstick. (See the recipe for details and illustrations.) A pastry marble, cut to fit your refrigerator shelf, is most desirable if you are going in for any serious pastry making. (Look in the Yellow Pages under Marble or Tombstones; the seller will cut one to size for you.) A heavy-duty electric mixer is the way to lightning-fast puff pastry; but, if you do it by hand, don't use a pastry blender for the new method. It cuts the butter too fine. Pleasant but nonessential aids are a roller-pricker and a large ravioli-cutting wheel.

A pastry bag with two cannelated (toothed) tubes, one medium-sized for the eggs, one tiny for the radishes, will prettify them.

An electric warming tray and a couple of portable cutting boards are a great help in serving, as are two or three wastebins with plastic trash-bag liners for the debris.

Marketing and Storage:
Staples to have on hand

Salt
Peppercorns
Granulated sugar
Orange bitters
Bottled sweetened lime juice
Hot pepper sauce, soy sauce, Worcestershire sauce
Capers
Orange marmalade
Oregano or thyme
Italian seasoning (an herb blend)
Mustard, the strong Dijon type (see page 5)
Tomato purée or sauce, canned

Olive oil or fresh new peanut oil
Garlic; shallots or scallions
Beef stock or bouillon, frozen or canned
Fresh bread crumbs (in the freezer; see
    page 5)
Wines and liqueurs: dry white French
    vermouth, Cognac, orange liqueur

Specific ingredients for this menu

Boiled ham (6 ounces or 180 g per Pithiviers)
Center-cut fresh salmon and/or other fresh
    fish (5 pounds or 2½ kg per recipe
    gravlaks) ▼
Fresh pork sausage meat (4 ounces or 115 g
    per recipe meatballs)
Lean ground beef (1 pound or 450 g per recipe
    meatballs)
Chicken wings (24 per recipe)
Small amounts (optional): fermented dry black
    Chinese beans; dark sesame oil; dried
    Chinese mushrooms; fresh or pickled
    ginger—for chicken wings ▼
Mayonnaise, anchovy paste, curry powder,
    and/or other items for stuffing hard-
    boiled eggs
Pumpernickel bread
Peanuts and/or various nuts, to serve with
    drinks
Heavy cream (4 Tb per Pithiviers)

Eggs (3 per Pithiviers, 1 for the meatballs, plus
    however many you wish for stuffed egg
    recipe)
Cheese for grating—Cheddar, Swiss, Parmesan
    or a combination of all three (1 pound or
    450 g at least; to be used for cheese
    appetizers and 6 ounces or 180 g per
    Pithiviers) ▼
Unsalted butter (2½ pounds or 1125 g for puff
    pastry, plus butter for pumpernickel
    bread, radishes, and other purposes)
Cake flour, plain bleached (1 cup or 140 g per
    puff pastry recipe)
All-purpose flour, unbleached (3 cups or 420 g
    per puff pastry recipe) ▼
Lemons (4 per chicken wing recipe, plus those
    needed for serving oysters and clams,
    drinks, etc.)
Limes, for drinks
Oranges (1 per apéritif recipe for 6 people)
Parsley and/or watercress, for decoration
Fresh or fragrant dried dill weed and, if
    available, spruce branches for *gravlaks* ▼
Radishes
Oysters and clams ▼
Ice cubes for drinks, and crushed ice for shellfish
Red wines, white wines, and dark Jamaica rum
Other drinks for your usual bar setup

▶ *Remarks:*

Fresh fish: be sure to buy the fish for your *gravlaks* well enough ahead—see recipe for details. *Fermented dry black Chinese beans and dark sesame oil:* obtainable in Chinese and Japanese grocery stores and many fancy food stores; good items to know because they add a very special flavor to all kinds of dishes, not only chicken, but shrimp, fish, and so forth. No reason to confine them to Oriental cooking. *Dried Chinese mushrooms:* you need only 2 or 3 of these pungent mushrooms to give a fine mushroom flavor to many a dish; soak them in warm water until they have softened, and if the stems remain tough, cut them off and discard them. Then slice or chop the mushrooms and use like fresh mushrooms. *Ginger:* fresh gingerroot is to be had in most supermarkets these days. You can freeze it and grate or slice it—still frozen—into whatever you are cooking, using just what you need and storing the rest in the freezer. Pickled ginger, put up in brine and usually vinegar, keeps for months in the refrigerator; you can normally find it in Japanese and Chinese grocery stores. *Cheese for grating:* I find it a very good idea to grate up leftover hard cheeses like Cheddar, Swiss, and Parmesan and to package them together in a plastic bag or container in my freezer; I always have cheese on hand, then, and none is wasted. *Unbleached all-purpose flour:* essential, in my experience, for puff pastry, since bleached flour makes a tough pastry and is also hard to roll out; if your market doesn't carry unbleached flour, look for it in health food stores. *Dill weed:* fresh dill is always preferable to dried when you can find it, and you can store it in your freezer: stem it, wash and dry it thoroughly, then chop it fine and pack it in small parcels for freezing. This works with chives too. The secret is to exclude all moisture and air before freezing. Sometimes you can find fragrant dried bottled dill weed; smell it before using to be sure it is full of flavor and aroma. *Oysters and clams:* see "Fish Talk," page 29, for details, including a clever way to open oysters.

A Preamble to French Puff Pastry— made a new fast way

The most marvelous of all doughs, to my mind, is French puff pastry, the pastry of a thousand leaves that puffs up in the oven as it bakes because it is made of many many layers of paper-thin dough interspersed with many many layers of butter. It is light as air, flaky, tender, buttery, and so good to eat just of itself that it hardly needs an accompaniment. It makes not only *vol-au-vent* pastry cases and patty shells, but all manner of tarts and cookies, cheese and ham concoctions, dessert cakes, and so forth. For a cocktail party it is practically a must, and, since you can prepare it months and months ahead, you could even consider it a staple ingredient to have on hand in your freezer. Once made, it can quickly be turned into a spectacular, like the ham Pithiviers to serve at this party—shown below just out of the oven.

I must admit to having spent years and years on puff pastry, starting out in Paris way back in the early 1950s. I learned to make it in the classical way, where you start with a flour-water dough that you spread out into a thick pancake and fold around an almost equal amount of butter. Next, you roll that out into

a long rectangle and the butter follows along inside the dough. Then you fold that into three, like a business letter, and roll it out again. All the time the butter is extending itself in layers inside the dough, and every time you fold it those layers triple in number until by the sixth roll-and-fold you have 729 layers of butter between 730 layers of dough.

All this manipulation gives the dough a heavy workout, which is fine when you have flour with a low gluten content, like French flour. But when you are working with regular American all-purpose flour, which has a relatively high gluten content, the dough becomes rubbery, refuses to be rolled out, and you have to let it rest and relax until you can continue. My French colleague Simone Beck and I almost gave up on *pâte feuilletée* with American flour until I happened to be doing a television show on entertaining at the White House, and their then pastry chef, Ferdinand Louvat, produced some splendid *vol-au-vent* structures. He used all-purpose flour, he told me, but for every 3 parts all-purpose flour he put in 1 part cake flour; the cake flour lowered the gluten content and made the dough easy to handle.

That was our first breakthrough, and the recipe for classic puff pastry using that formula is in Volume II of *Mastering*. The second breakthrough is an entirely new way of making the pastry, suggested by a reading of *La Cuisine de Denis* (ed. Robert Laffont, Paris, 1975). Instead of forming the dough into a package encasing a mass of butter, you break the butter up into large pieces the size of lima beans and mix them with the flour, salt, and water; then you form this messy-looking mass into a long rectangle, patting and rolling it out. You fold it into three, roll it out, fold it again, and it begins to look like dough. After 2 additional turns it is smooth and fine; you then rest it 40 minutes and it is ready for its final 2 rolls and folds and its forming and baking. Now puff pastry can be made in an hour, rather than the 3 or 4 hours usually necessary for the classical method using all-purpose flour.

Because the butter is in large lumps, they form themselves into the required layers as you proceed to roll and fold the dough. You can see from the illustrations that the puff pastry rises dramatically as it should—just as much as if not more so than the classical puff pastry. In fact, since experimenting with this new system I've not gone back to the old method at all.

Puff pastry proportions

Proportions for the new fast puff pastry are 5 parts butter to 4 parts flour—the large amount of butter necessary because you have to flour the dough more as you roll it than in the old method. These amounts easily translate into metrics as 125 grams butter for every 100 grams flour. In cups and spoons they approximate:

1 cup (5 ounces or 140 g) flour as follows:
    ¾ cup (3½ ounces or 105 g) unbleached all-purpose flour, and
    ¼ cup (1¼ ounces or 35 g) plain bleached cake flour

1½ sticks plus 1 Tb (6½ ounces or 185 g) chilled unsalted butter
Scant ½ tsp salt
¼ cup (½ dL) iced water

Hand versus machine

I like to make my pastry in a heavy-duty electric mixer with flat beater, using 4 cups of flour and ending up with a goodly amount of dough. It does not work well in a food processor, because the butter becomes too much broken up and the pastry does not puff dramatically. Mixing by hand works out nicely, but be sure not to soften the butter too much; cut it into ½-inch dice, then rub it with the flour between the balls of your fingers until it is broken into thickish disks, like fat cornflakes. The water goes in after the butter and flour have been mixed together, making a very rough, barely cohesive mass.

Fast French Puff Pastry

Pâte Feuilletée Exprès

For one 9-inch Pithiviers and 36 or more cheese appetizers; or for a rectangle of dough some 36 by 12 by ¼ inches (90 x 30 x ¾ cm)

Note: Measure flour by dipping dry-measure cups into container, then sweeping off excess even with lip of cup; no sifting necessary.

3 cups (420 g) unbleached all-purpose flour
1 cup (140 g) plain bleached cake flour
6½ sticks (26 ounces or 735 g) chilled unsalted butter
1½ tsp salt
1 cup (¼ L) iced water
Equipment
A heavy-duty electric mixer with flat beater (useful); a 1½-by-2-foot (45-x-60-cm) work surface, preferably of marble; a rolling pin at least 16 inches (40 cm) long; a pastry sheet (for lifting and turning dough) about 10 inches (25 cm) wide; a pastry scraper or wide spatula; plastic wrap

Mixing the dough

Place the flour in your mixing bowl. Rapidly cut the sticks of chilled butter into lengthwise quarters, then into ½-inch (1½-cm) dice; * add to the flour—if you have taken too long to cut the butter and if it has softened, refrigerate bowl to chill butter before proceeding. Add the salt. Blend flour and butter together rapidly, if by hand to make large flakes about an inch in size. By machine the butter should be roughly broken up but stay in lumps the size of large lima beans. Blend in the water, mixing just enough so that dough masses roughly together but butter pieces remain about the same size.

The first 4 turns

Turn dough out onto a lightly floured work surface, as illustrated in the first picture on the right. Rapidly push and pat and roll it out into a rectangle in front of you—12 to 14 inches for 2 cups of flour, about 18 for 4 cups (30 to 35 cm and 40 to 45 cm). It will look an awful mess! Lightly flour top of dough and, with pastry sheet to help you, flip bottom of rectangle up over the middle, and then flip the top down to cover it, as though folding a business letter. Lift dough off work surface with pastry sheet; scrape work surface clean, flour the surface lightly, and return dough to it, settling it down in front of you so that the top flap is at your right. Lightly flour top of dough, and pat, push, and roll it out again into a rectangle; it will look a little less messy. Fold again into three as before—each of these roll-and-fold operations is called a "turn." Roll out and fold 2 more times, making 4 turns in all, and by the last one the pastry should actually look like dough. You should see large flakes of butter scattered under the surface of the dough, which is just as it should be. With the balls of your fingers (not your fingernails) make 4

If you have bought the kind of butter that seems soft and sweats water when you cut it, that means it is inferior quality and will not make this puff pastry rise as it should. In this case you eliminate the extra moisture by first kneading it in ice water and then squeezing in a damp towel to remove excess water. Then chill.

depressions in the dough to indicate the 4 turns, as I've done in the final picture below—just in case you go off and forget what you've done.

Finishing the dough—the 2 final turns
Wrap the dough in plastic, place in a plastic bag, and refrigerate for 40 minutes (or longer) to firm the butter and relax the gluten in the dough. Give the dough 2 more turns, beating it back and forth and up and down first if chilled and hard. Let dough rest another 30 minutes if it seems rubbery and hard to roll; then it is ready for forming and baking.

🕐 Dough may be frozen after the first 4 turns, although it is easier to complete the 6 of them before freezing. It will keep, wrapped airtight, for months. Defrost overnight in the refrigerator, or at room temperature.

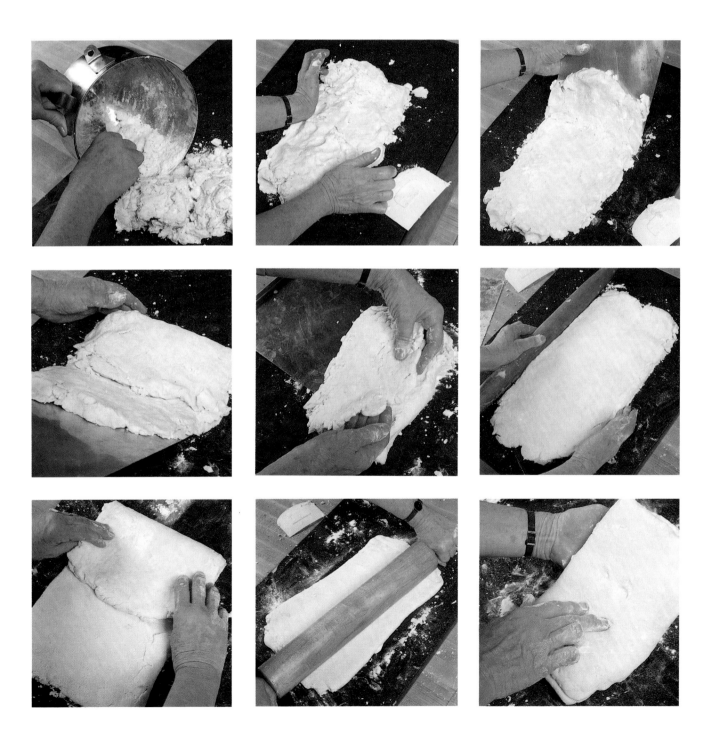

Ham Pithiviers

Puff pastry tart with ham filling

For a 9½-inch (24-cm) tart serving 8 to 10 generously, or 20 cocktail bites

⅔ previous puff pastry (cut after rolling out, as described in this recipe)

6 ounces (180 g) best-quality boiled ham

2 Tb butter

2 Tb minced shallots or scallions

2 egg yolks

¼ cup (½ dL) heavy cream

Drops of Worcestershire sauce

Drops of hot pepper sauce

Freshly ground pepper

6 Tb freshly grated Parmesan, Swiss, and/or Cheddar cheese

Egg glaze (1 egg beaten with 1 tsp water)

Equipment

(In addition to items suggested for puff pastry recipe above): a baking sheet, round nonstick pizza tray recommended; a roller-pricker, or two table forks; a pastry brush

The ham filling

Cut the ham into thin irregular slices about 1 by 1 by ⅛ inches (2½ x 2½ x ½ cm) and sauté briefly in the butter with the shallots or scallions, just to warm through thoroughly. Remove from heat. In a small bowl, beat the egg yolks with the cream; stir this mixture into the ham along with drops of Worcestershire and pepper sauce and freshly ground pepper to taste. Warm over low heat, folding the ham into the sauce, until it thickens but does not boil. Set aside to cool and thicken even more. It should be cold when it goes into the Pithiviers.

🕐 Filling may be prepared in advance and refrigerated.

Forming the dough

Roll the dough (the whole of the recipe) out into a rectangle about 18 by 9 inches (45 x 20 cm) and cut into thirds crosswise; refrigerate 2 pieces, wrapping and storing one of them for another use. Roll remaining piece, which will be the bottom of the tart, into a square 12 inches (30 cm) to a side; using a pie plate or cake pan to guide you, cut a 9½-inch (24-cm) disk out of the center of the dough. Remove surrounding dough and set on a baking sheet for reconstituting later. Lightly fold disk in

half and set upside down on dampened baking surface. Roll out second piece of dough to a thickness of slightly more than ¼ inch (¾ cm)—it must be this thickness to puff dramatically—and cut it into a disk the same size as the first. Refrigerate it along with the surrounding dough pieces from both disks.

● Dough disks may be formed and stored in the freezer.

Assembling the Pithiviers
With the balls of your fingers, push and pat bottom disk of dough out onto its baking surface to make an even circle slightly larger than your cutting guide. With a roller-pricker or two forks, prick dough all over at ½-inch (1½-cm) intervals, going down through dough to pastry sheet to keep this bottom layer from rising too much. Form the ham into a round cake, about 4½ to 5 inches (12 to 13 cm) across—layers of ham interspersed with

sprinklings of cheese—and place in the center of the dough. It is important to leave a 2-inch (5-cm) border of clear dough all around the ham to prevent leakage of filling during baking. Paint border of dough with cold water, and immediately center top layer in place, stretching gently as necessary. With a sharp-pointed knife, make a little hole ⅛ inch (½ cm) wide in the center of the dough, going down into the filling, to allow for escaping steam during baking. Then, with the ball of your first three fingers, firmly press the two pieces of dough in place all around. (Dough should probably be chilled at this point, but if it is still firm, proceed to the scalloped edging described in next step, then chill it.)

● May be wrapped airtight and frozen at this point, or after its scalloped edging. May then be decorated and baked, still in its frozen state.

Decorating the Pithiviers

Preheat oven to 450° F/230°C, and set rack in lower middle level. Make a scalloped edging around the Pithiviers as follows: set an upturned bowl slightly smaller than the Pithiviers over it, and use it as a guide in cutting 2-inch-wide (5-cm) scallops all around the circumference; decorate their edges all around by pressing upright lines against them with the back of a knife. Just before putting it in the oven, and after making sure top of dough is chilled and firm, paint the top with a film of egg glaze; then wait a moment and paint with a second film of glaze. Finally, with the point of a small knife, cut decorative lines 1/16 inch (¼ cm) deep in the top of the dough. A typical pattern is curving lines from center to edge, like the spokes of a wheel; or trace 4 long ovals from center to edge with straight line down the center and shallow crosshatch marks in between.

Baking, holding, serving

Baking time: 45 to 60 minutes

Immediately set the Pithiviers in the preheated oven and bake for about 20 minutes, until it has puffed and is beginning to brown nicely—it should rise dramatically, to a height of at least 2 inches (5 cm). Turn oven down to 400°F/200°C and bake 20 to 30 minutes more, watching it does not brown too much—cover loosely with foil if it does, and turn thermostat a little lower if you think it necessary. Baking takes longer than you might think, since all the pastry layers should cook and crisp. The Pithiviers should be done when the sides feel quite firm; to be sure, turn oven off and leave the Pithiviers in for another 10 to 15 minutes. You may keep it in a warming oven or on an electric hot tray for an hour or more, but the sooner you serve it the more tenderly flaky and delicious it will be. To serve, with a serrated knife simply cut into wedges like a pie.

Puffed Cheese Appetizers

Reconstituted leftover puff pastry dough
You can easily turn the fresh leftovers of your unused dough back into first-class puff pastry as follows: keep the bits and pieces all in one flat layer and glue them together by wetting the edge of one piece with cold water, laying the edge of another piece on top, and so on until you have made a patchwork mat of dough. Roll it with your pin, and give it 2 turns (rollings and foldings into three). If you want to use it plain, give it 2 more turns, but to transform it into cheese appetizers, roll it out into a rectangle, and for a piece 12 by 14 inches (30 x 35 cm), spread about 4 tablespoons grated cheese across the middle. Flip bottom of dough over to cover it, spread more cheese on that upturned portion, and flip the top third of the dough over to cover it. Repeat with another roll-out and cheese fold-up, then roll out the dough into a rectangle slightly thicker than ¼ inch (¾ cm). Cut into strips 2 inches (5 cm) wide—if too narrow the appetizers will topple

over as they rise in the oven. Then cut into lengths 3 inches (8 cm) long and set on a baking sheet.

🕐 May be wrapped and frozen at this point.

Just before baking, preheat oven to 450°F/230°C, paint tops of pieces with egg glaze, and sprinkle on a layer of grated cheese. Bake about 15 minutes, until appetizers have puffed and browned. Best kept warm until serving time, but they can be frozen and reheated, still frozen.

Gravlaks

Dilled fresh salmon (or sea bass)

For a 5-pound center cut of fish, boned (thus in two large halves or fillets), with skin intact

Spruce branches (if available)

2½ Tb salt and 1¼ Tb sugar mixed in a small bowl

Large bunch fresh dill weed, or 1½ Tb fragrant dried dill weed

4 to 5 Tb Cognac

Equipment

A porcelain, enamel, or glass dish, just large enough to hold fish comfortably; wax paper or plastic wrap; a plate or board that will just fit inside dish; a 5-pound (2-kg) weight

Rub fingers over the flesh to locate any bones that may still remain; salmon fillets often have small bones running slantwise from top to bottom of the thick side of the flesh. Remove with pliers.

If you have fresh spruce, cut enough twigs to cover the bottom of the dish and arrange a layer of fresh dill on top. Lay one fillet of fish skin side down in the dish and the other skin side down on your work surface. Rub the flesh sides of each fillet with the salt and sugar mixture and the dried dill if you are not using fresh. Sprinkle on the Cognac. (If you are using fresh dill, arrange a layer over the fish in the dish.) Place second fillet over first, flesh to flesh, but reversing its direction so that the thick or backbone part of the second fillet is resting against the thin or belly part of the first. Cover with more fresh dill and spruce twigs if you have them. Spread paper or plastic over the fish and the plate or board, and weight. Refrigerate for 2 days, basting with liquid in dish two or three times. After 2 days, taste by slicing a bit of fish off; add a teaspoon or so more salt if you feel it is not salty enough, and perhaps a sprinkling of Cognac. Reverse the fish so bottom fillet will be on top and return to refrigerator with board and weight for another 2 to 3 days, making 4 to 5 days in all. Taste carefully; the fish should now be ready to eat.

To serve

Set a fillet skin side down on a board and with a very sharp, long knife, start 4 to 5 inches (10 to 13 cm) from larger end of fillet and make paper-thin slices toward the tail, with your knife almost parallel to the board.

Remarks:

For a quicker cure, 3 to 4 days at most, you may slice your fish before curing and arrange in slightly overlapping layers, lightly salted and dilled, until the dish is full. Cover, weight, and refrigerate as before.

🕐   Dilled fish will keep for 10 days to 2 weeks under refrigeration.

Minimeatballs

For 40 to 50 meatballs about 1 inch (2 ½ cm) in diameter

½ cup (4 ounces or 115 g) pork sausage meat

2 cups (1 pound or 450 g) lean ground beef

1 egg

⅔ cup (1 ½ dL) fresh nonsweet white bread crumbs soaked in 5 Tb dry white French vermouth

2 cloves garlic, puréed

8 drops hot pepper sauce

2 tsp soy sauce

1 tsp salt

8 grinds black pepper

½ tsp oregano or thyme

Flour (for dredging)

Serving sauce

1 cup (¼ L) beef stock or bouillon

1 tsp soy sauce

2 Tb Dijon-type strong prepared mustard beaten to blend with ½ cup (1 dL) dry white French vermouth

Salt, pepper, and oregano or thyme

2 Tb tomato purée or sauce (optional)

Beat meat, egg, crumbs, and seasonings together, using a food processor if you want a very smooth mixture. Roll gobs into balls 1 inch (2 ½ cm) in diameter; roll lightly in flour, and arrange in one layer in a lightly oiled baking dish or jelly-roll pan. Bake in a preheated 450°F/230°C oven in upper middle level, 7 to 8 minutes, turning once or twice, to brown nicely and just to stiffen. Drain in a sieve or a colander. Boil down the ingredients for the sauce until lightly thickened, carefully correct seasoning, and fold in the minimeatballs.

At serving time, reheat and place in a casserole on an electric warming device, or in an electric frying pan on lowest heat. Have a jar of toothpicks close by.

Peking Wings

Sautéed chicken wings with Oriental overtones

24 chicken wings, folded akimbo
4 lemons
4 thin slices fresh or pickled ginger (optional)
2 Tb soy sauce
½ cup (½ dL) olive oil or fresh peanut oil
1 tsp dark sesame oil (optional)
1 tsp thyme or Italian seasoning
4 large cloves fresh garlic, puréed
½ tsp cracked peppercorns
Salt and pepper
Fresh minced parsley (optional)
Optional Oriental touches, to be added to pan after chicken has browned
2 Tb fermented dry black Chinese beans
Handful of dried Chinese mushrooms, softened in warm water, stemmed, and sliced

Marinating the chicken

Dry off the chicken in paper towels and place in a stainless-steel bowl. Zest 2 lemons (remove yellow part of peel with a vegetable peeler), and cut zest into julienne (matchstick) strips along with the optional ginger. Add both to the chicken as well as strained juice of 2 lemons, the soy sauce, 4 tablespoons oil, the optional sesame oil, the thyme or Italian seasoning, the garlic, and the peppercorns. Turn and baste the chicken. Marinate for 2 hours or longer in the refrigerator, turning and basting several times. Just before cooking, scrape marinade off chicken and back into bowl. Pat chicken dry in paper towels.

Cooking the chicken

(The wings are first browned, then simmered in their marinade liquid.) Film a large frying pan with oil and heat to very hot but not smoking; then brown on all sides as many chicken wings as will fit easily in one layer, remove, and brown the rest. When all chicken wings are browned, lower heat and return them to pan with the marinade ingredients and optional black beans and mushrooms; cover, and simmer. Meanwhile, slice remaining lemons thin; carefully remove seeds. After 10 minutes, turn the chicken and baste with the accumulated juices; spread the lemon slices over the chicken.

🕐   You may complete the recipe to this point, uncover the chicken, and set aside until 10 minutes or so before you wish to serve.

Continue cooking the chicken slowly 8 to 10 minutes longer, or until tender when pierced with a small knife; baste several times during this final cooking. Correct seasoning; if you wish, sprinkle parsley over the chicken, and the wings are ready to serve. Transfer to an electric heating device (or an electric frying pan) along with the cooking juices and keep over low heat.

Oysters and Clams:
See illustrated directions for opening them, as well as directions for buying and storing them, in "Fish Talk," page 29.

Stuffed Eggs:
Hard-boil and peel eggs. For a party like this I like a quite simple filling made of sieved yolks flavored with salt, pepper, homemade mayonnaise, and a little anchovy paste, lemon, capers, or curry powder, and no recipe is needed for this. However, I do think eggs look most attractive and professional when filled with a pastry bag and cannelated tube.

Buttered Radishes:
Combining the bland and peppery flavors of butter and radishes is very French. A pretty way is to cut radish roses, let them spread out overnight in a bowl of iced water, hollow the white tops a bit with a knife point, and pipe in a little squirt of beaten unsalted butter. Chill again in iced water and serve in plenty of crushed ice to keep the topknots stiff.

A la Recherche de l'Orange Perdue

Paul Child's rum and orange cocktail
For 6 cocktail-size drinks, using jigger measurement of 1 ½ ounces

2 jiggers (6 Tb) dark Jamaica rum

½ jigger (2 tsp) bottled sweetened lime juice

Juice of 1 lime

½ jigger (2 tsp) orange liqueur

1 Tb orange marmalade

3 jiggers (9 Tb) dry white French vermouth

1 whole orange, quartered

5 shakes orange bitters

6 ice cubes

Place all ingredients in jar of electric blender and blend 20 seconds. Strain through a sieve into a pitcher. Cover and refrigerate until serving time. Stir before serving, and pour into chilled cocktail glasses.

🕐 *Timing*

There are no last-minute jobs for this party, since you open the oysters and clams as you serve them. We find, too, that people enjoy doing their own, by the surefire method described on pages 31 to 32.

Cook the chicken wings that afternoon for best flavor; but if you do want to do it earlier, peel off as much skin as you can right after cooking—that's where the reheated flavor seems to lodge. It's so difficult to keep the stuffed eggs from darkening and drying that I usually pipe in the stuffing (prepared earlier and covered closely) just before the party; but you could do it that morning and sprinkle the tops with finely minced chives, parsley, or ham.

Puff pastry is at its glorious best served fresh from the oven, but you can make, shape, and freeze the dough months in advance, make and refrigerate the ham filling a day early, and assemble the pastries in the morning. Keep chilled until you bake them.

Cut the radish roses the night before, refrigerate them in iced water, stuff them in the morning, and put them back in more iced water.

Oysters and clams keep very well properly packed and refrigerated; buy them a day or two beforehand and store unopened.

Gravlaks, if you're doing it in two pieces, must be started almost a week beforehand and tasted after two days to see how it's doing. If you slice it before salting, three or four days should suffice.

Menu Variations

Puff pastry: The possibilities are limitless—see *Mastering II* and *J.C.'s Kitchen* for many good ideas.

Gravlaks: I find the method for *gravlaks* works beautifully for sea bass and bluefish, and often, as in this menu, I like to serve two kinds. A warning: sole (perhaps because it is so lean) is, I think, less successful in taste and texture.

Peking wings: Using the same general cooking techniques, you could substitute small drumsticks for chicken wings, or pieces of boned chicken breast served on toothpicks.

Oysters and clams: If you don't like your shellfish raw, you can make a noble presentation by boiling a monster lobster, cooling it, and serving the meat, cut in chunks, in the shell. It is simply an old wives' tale that large lobsters are tough. They're delicious.

These are Cotuit oysters from Cape Cod.

Leftovers

Puff pastry: The Pithiviers and the cheese appetizers can be frozen and reheated. Although they will never have quite their glorious original taste, they will still make very good eating.

Gravlaks: Will keep for ten days or so under refrigeration. As to using it hot, I find it very salty if baked or broiled—a good illustration that you oversalt cold dishes slightly, and should exercise restraint with hot ones. However, I have used it in a creamy fish soup, as part of a quiche mixture, with creamed potatoes, and as part of a fish stuffing, since in these cases the surrounding ingredients draw the salt out of the salmon. One has to be careful, of course, not to salt anything else because of the salmon's salt.

Minimeatballs: These can be reheated, or served cold with sliced onions, tomatoes, cucumbers, and so forth. Or you can chop them and add to a hearty soup.

Peking wings: These are delicious cold, but if you want to reheat them, skin them first. The meat is good in a salad, sandwich, or soup.

Oysters and clams: These will keep unopened in the refrigerator for a week or more. They are delicious broiled on the half shell, or in a stew or chowder.

Postscript

I can't leave this cocktail party without again extolling the virtues of French puff pastry. It is now, with this fast method, so easy to make and is so infinitely versatile that I always have a hefty package of it on hand in my freezer. After one television bout some years ago, I kept several batches of it for two years! It thawed, rolled out, and baked just as beautifully as anyone could wish when I finally exhumed it. If you enjoy pastry making, this is a very satisfying dough, all neat and squared when you get the turns going, and it lends elegance to any menu. It even sounds nice when you break or bite into it—something between a crackle, a crunch, and a rustle, like a fire as it kindles.

For centuries of thrifty peasants, for eminent gastronomes —and for your own hungry horde

Cassoulet for a Crowd

Menu
For 10 to 12 people

Consommé au Porto
Toasted Armenian Cracker Bread

❧

Cassoulet —Beans baked with goose, lamb,
and sausages
Pickled Red Cabbage Slaw
Hot French Bread

❧

Sliced Fresh Pineapple—En Boat

❧

Suggested wines:
A hearty red with the cassoulet—Burgundy,
Côtes du Rhône, pinot noir, zinfandel

Cassoulet, that best of bean feasts, is every-day fare for a peasant but ambrosia for a gastronome, though its ideal consumer is a 300-pound blocking back who has been splitting firewood nonstop for the last twelve hours on a subzero day in Manitoba. It feeds a lot of people and can be made a day or even two days in advance, with much preparation done even before that, so, when the Child household is expecting a horde of peasants, gastronomes, and blocking backs, cassoulet is what they'll get. Sunrise smiles break out as they come through our door, for the whole house is filled with a full-bodied, earthy fragrance. In every heart the joyous resolution forms: "I am now going to eat myself silly."

It's a mighty dish, with its fragments of rich meats, its golden-brown juice thick with starch from the beans, its top crunchy and flecked with green (and with bits of pork rind, if you decide to use it). But the great thing is the wonderful taste of the beans, which absorb and blend the complex savors of the well-seasoned meats. And there is a mysterious charm in how, by long cooking, a stony little white bean becomes pale amber, redolent, swollen, velvety. Eating one bean at a time, crushing it against the palate, you could make a career of, and some cassoulet buffs apparently do.

Many of us have been privileged to witness the uproarious kangaroo court that all bystanders rush to join whenever one French motorist so much as nudges another.

If you can imagine this in full cry for two centuries, you will know what is implied by the Great, Ancient, Passionate, 98 Percent Fact-Free Cassoulet Controversy that still rages unabated. Three neighboring hill towns north of the Pyrenees in Languedoc define this small battleground, but the hullabaloo is audible all over the world. The January 1979 issue of the *International Review of Food and Wine* neatly summarized and simplified the conflicts of the past as follows: "In Castelnaudary, the legend goes, the dish was invented, and therefore a 'pure' version is served. The haricots are cooked with chunks of fresh pork, pork knuckle, ham, pork sausage, and fresh pork rind. In Toulouse the cooks add Toulouse sausage and either *confit d'oie* or *confit de canard* (preserved goose or duck), while in Carcassonne chunks of mutton are added to the Castelnaudary formula, and, during the hunting season, an occasional partridge too." Clear enough, but in the course of their research the authors of this article, William Bayer and Paula Wolfert, soon found that "these regional distinctions are now completely blurred, and that cassoulet, like life itself, is not so simple as it seems."

Mr. Bayer and Ms. Wolfert had traveled to the battlefront for a restaurant tour, with the sensible object of reporting not on the "original" cassoulet or the "definitive" one, both mythical anyway, but simply on the versions they liked best. Their favorite turned out to be a radical-revisionist one using *fresh* beans, favas. I recommend their article to admirers of sound, felicitous food writing as well as to cassoulet fanatics, who will enjoy pondering both the unusual fava formula and another Toulousain type that turned out, after much sampling, to be the authors' favorite of the traditional recipes.

My own current version, the fourth I've developed, is a selection and synthesis of traditional methods and components, but in fact you can use almost anything you have handy in making cassoulet, and I'm sure the

cooks of Languedoc have always done likewise. So why such a fuss? Partly, I think, because the instruments so inspire the imagination that any creative cook is periodically compelled to reorchestrate them. And partly because a fuss is a very French way to have fun.

My efforts have tended toward a progressively lighter and leaner dish, as I see looking back at the recipes in *Mastering I, The French Chef Cookbook,* and *J.C.'s Kitchen,* which has a quickie version using lentils. Even so, this cassoulet remains hearty indeed. What to eat with it is no problem, since its full flavors need no rounding out or complement. You just want something assertive for contrast and, given the main dish's rather stolid quality, something very light. Nothing sharpens appetites like a perfect, crystalline consommé, and with that I like the crackly crunch of storebought Armenian flatbread, crisped in the oven. For a juicy crunch, and for an offset to stodge, suavity,

Cassoulet country centers around Toulouse, Carcassonne, and Castelnaudary.

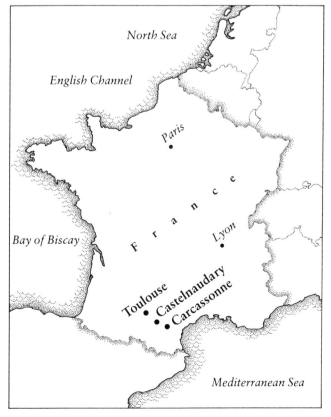

and succulence, the cassoulet is accompanied here by pickled red cabbage and hot French bread. Fresh pineapple, honey-sweet but with that haunting acid tang, is an ideal dessert if you can find fruit that were harvested when perfectly ripe. (For clues, and a bit of debunking, see Remarks later in this chapter.)

Some cooks say they serve cassoulet only to joggers and only at midday, so they can run it off before bedtime. I like it any time at all, but especially on the eve of that movable and dire feast (joke) which opens the Season of Nemesis. Hail, Cassoulet! We who are about to diet salute you.

A Note on Beans and Intestinal Motility:

Intestinal motility is polite gobbledegook for flatulence, which in turn means gas. What about that problem and beans? It seems, according to scientists at the Western Regional Center in Albany, California, that beans contain the difficult-to-digest sugars, stachyose and raffinose. The human body does not have the enzymes to break them down, and when these culprits reach the lower intestine of some diners, their resident bacteria react violently, producing gas or, in a word, motility.

The good news, however, is that these same scientists have discovered you can boil 1 cup (¼ L) beans in 10 cups (2½ L) water for 3 minutes, soak them for 10 hours or overnight in the same water, drain and rinse them, and set them to cook in fresh water. This, they assure us, eliminates 80 percent of the trouble.

P.S.: This account came from a newspaper report, but in later correspondence with Alfred Olson, leader of the U.S.D.A.'s bean study group, he writes that he has changed the word "motility"—although he likes the sound of it, he is not sure of its accuracy in this connection, and has regretfully substituted the more prosaic but possibly more safely descriptive "trouble."

Preparations and Marketing

Recommended Equipment:

For clarifying the consommé, you need sieving equipment—cheesecloth for lining an 8- to 10-inch (20- to 25-cm) sieve, a colander to rest the sieve over, and a bowl into which the consommé can drip freely.

For the cassoulet you need a 6-quart (6-L) flameproof baking-serving dish or casserole, illustrated on page 63. You will want an 8-quart (7- to 8-L) pot in which to boil the beans before they go into the casserole.

For preserving the goose you'll need a big bowl or crock in which the cut-up goose pieces may sit during their salting, and something the size of a preserving kettle or stockpot for rendering the fat and then for cooking the goose. If you plan to put the goose down for storage in its own fat, you will want a crock or bowl large enough to hold the cooked goose pieces, and to fit into your refrigerator, plus a rack that will fit in the bottom. A deep-fat-frying thermometer is useful here.

To shred the red cabbage very fine indeed, a shredding or sauerkraut cutter is useful, or a very sharp knife and a practiced hand. The knife is also needed for the pineapples.

Marketing Note: If you are to preserve your own goose for this menu, you will be starting from twenty-four hours to several weeks in advance, so I have marked the items for goose preservation with an asterisk on the lists.

Staples to Have on Hand:

Salt
Sugar
Optional: coarse or kosher salt or sea salt
Black peppercorns
Ground allspice and thyme

Mustard seeds
Juniper berries
Imported bay leaves
Optional: dried tarragon
Tomato sauce (page 111) or tomato paste
Beef stock or bouillon (at least 3 cups or ¾ L)
Meat or poultry stock, or a mixture of canned
    chicken broth and canned consommé
    (2 quarts or 2 L)
Optional: more stock or consommé
Gelatin
Butter or cooking oil
Yellow onions (3 large)
Dry white wine or dry white French vermouth

Optional: white rum or kirsch
Port wine
Red-wine vinegar

Specific Ingredients for This Menu:

* Optional: saltpeter (from a pharmacy)
* "Roaster" goose (10 to 12 pounds or 4½ to
    5½ kg) or preserved goose (3 pounds or
    1350 g) ▼
Cooking sausage, like kielbasy, chorizo, or
    sausage meat (1½ to 2 pounds or 675 to
    900 g)
Bone-in lamb shoulder (about 4 pounds or 2
    kg), sawed into stewing chunks

Optional: salt pork, fat-and-lean type, with
  rind (1 pound or 450 g)
* Fresh pork fat and/or lard (about 1 pound or
  450 g)
  Dried white beans (2 pounds or 900 g) ▼
  Red onion (1 large)
  Parsley (1 large bunch)
  Optional: fresh mint
  Garlic (1 large head)
  Red cabbage (1 head fresh)
  Optional: sweet red bell pepper (1 large)
  Optional: small quantities of aromatic vegeta-
    bles like celery, onion, leek, carrot
  Tart apples (4)
  Pineapples (2 to 4, depending on size) ▼
  Canned beet juice, or borscht (½ cup or 1 dL)
  Egg whites (5)
  Nonsweet white French or Italian bread (½
    loaf)
  Armenian Cracker Bread

▶ **Remarks:**

Preserved goose (confit d'oie), if you don't
want to make your own, may be bought in
cans at the fancier "gourmet" shops. If you
can't get it, don't give up having cassoulet, as
several substitutions are possible (see Menu
Variations). *The goose:* you will probably
have to buy it frozen, and geese freeze well
when kept properly, at a constant temperature below −5°F/−20°C for no more than
six months. Defrost it either for several days
in the refrigerator (in its plastic package), or
in a tub of cold water (in its package), where
it will take 4 to 5 hours. Plan to use it within
a day of its defrosting. *Dry white beans:* I
use the medium bean, Great Northern, but
small white pea beans will do nicely, too.
Pineapples: I have learned so much myself,
since our encounter with them preparing this
dinner, that I think they deserve a special
place here. Now, praises be, thanks to modern refrigeration and fast transportation, it is
possible to buy field-ripened fresh sweet pineapple anywhere in this country. As a matter of fact, if it was not picked ripe in the
first place, it will not ripen at all because of
the way the pineapple is built: the fruit gets

its nourishment from the stump of the plant
on which it grows, and when the starch in
the stump turns to sugar, the sugar moves up
into the fruit and that is what ripens and
sweetens the pineapple. Once it is cut off
from its stump, its sugar supply ceases, and it
cannot, physically, get any sweeter. It will
lose some of its acidity if you keep it for a
few days at room temperature, but its sweet-
ness—or lack of it—was predetermined the
moment it was picked. Obviously, then, we
need good pickers in those pineapple fields,
and we want to buy from shippers who
know their pickers, and from merchants who
are well aware of the whole pineapple syn-
drome. As usual, it is up to us, the buying
public, to heckle our markets into providing
us with the fine, ripe, large, sweet pineapples
that they can procure for us—and they can,
we know it.

A ripe pineapple has a sweet pineapple aroma.

But how to tell, when buying a pineapple in a strange place, that it is sweet and ripe? First, you'll have your best luck in full pineapple season, when they are at their peak, from April through June. Color is no indication of ripeness, because a fine sweet specimen can vary from green to greenish yellow to yellow. Pulling a green leaf out of the crown doesn't mean a thing, nor does the sound of the thumping thumb. Probably the best test is the nose test—does it smell sweetly like a nice ripe pineapple? Aroma can be difficult to pick up if the pineapple has been chilled, but a faint perfume should exude even so.

Choose the largest fruits you can find—the bigger they are, the more flesh. The whole fruit should look fresh and healthy, with no leaking juices, bleary eyes, or soft spots. The crown of leaves should be freshly green and smartly upstanding. If the pineapple does not seem quite as ripe as it could be, keep it in a shady spot at normal room temperature for a few days, which should help it lose some of its acidity. Then, when it smells ripe (but do not let it soften and spoil), refrigerate it in a plastic bag, and plan to eat it as soon as you can.

By the way, when you have sliced up your pineapple but left the crown intact, you can plant the crown and grow yourself a pineapple plant like the one in the photograph. Slice off the top ½ inch (1½ cm) with the crown of leaves, says our gardening expert Jim Crockett, and scrape out the flesh. Let the crown dry in the sun for 2 weeks, then plant it in potting soil 2 inches (5 cm) deep and leave in a warm sunny place. Keep it barely moist and it will grow and produce a baby pineapple—presumably even if you have a black rather than a green thumb. (I have never grown one myself, but the one pictured here was grown indoors during the coldest January and February known in Massachusetts for almost 50 years—so there's living proof it can be done.)

Clear Consommé au Porto

The term "a clear consommé" means a perfectly clear, see-through sparkling dark amber liquid. It is a rare meat stock, bouillon, or canned consommé that can meet these requirements, and if you want them you will have to clarify a soup yourself. It's a quite magical process anyway and a most useful one to know when you need not only a perfect consommé, but aspic to coat a cold fish or a chicken or a poached egg.

For about 2 quarts (2 L)

2 quarts (2 L) meat or poultry stock, or canned chicken broth and canned consommé

Salt and pepper as needed

5 egg whites

Optional for added flavor: 4 Tb each minced celery, onion, leek if available, carrot, parsley stems, and ½ tsp dried tarragon

1 cup (¼ L) dry white wine or dry white French vermouth, or another cup of stock

4 Tb or more Port wine

Equipment:

A large sieve lined with 5 thicknesses of washed cheesecloth, set over a colander set over a bowl (colander must be large enough so its bottom will not rest in the consommé to come); a ladle

Before you begin, be sure that your meat stock, homemade or canned, is thoroughly free of fat or grease, and the same for all of your equipment—otherwise your clarification may not succeed.

Bring all but 1 cup of the stock to the simmer in a large saucepan; correct seasoning. Meanwhile, whip the egg whites lightly in a bowl and mix thoroughly with the 1 cup stock, optional flavoring ingredients, and wine. When stock is simmering, dribble 2 cups (½ L) of it slowly into the egg whites, beating all the while. Then beat the egg white mixture into the pan of hot stock. Set over moderate heat and, stirring slowly but reaching everywhere throughout the liquid with a wire whip, bring just to the simmer. Do not stir again. (Stock is constantly stirred so that egg whites will be thoroughly distributed and will draw to themselves all the cloudy particles in the stock, until simmer is reached.) Set saucepan at side of heat and let it almost simmer at one point for 5 minutes; rotate the pan ⅓ turn and let almost simmer another 5 minutes; rotate again, and repeat the process. (This coagulates the egg whites so that they will have enough body to hold themselves back when stock is strained.)

Gently and carefully ladle stock and egg whites into the lined sieve, letting the clear liquid drip through undisturbed. When dripping has ceased, remove straining contraption to another bowl and gently squeeze cheesecloth to extract a little more. If it is perfectly clear, pour it into the rest. Continue, stopping when the slightest suggestion of cloudiness appears.

Pour the Port wine into the clear soup by spoonfuls to taste, and the consommé is ready to serve or to reheat.

🕐   May be prepared in advance. When cool, cover and refrigerate or freeze.

Jellied Consommé:

For each 3 cups (¾ L) of consommé desired, soften 1 envelope (1 Tb) plain unflavored gelatin in ¼ cup (½ dL) cold soup or white wine or vermouth. Then heat it with ½ cup (1 dL) or so consommé until completely dissolved; stir into the rest of the consommé. Chill until set, then spoon into chilled consommé cups.

Aspic:

Use the same system as above for making aspics, but with the following proportions. However, always test your aspic consistency before using: pour 1 tablespoon aspic into a saucer, chill until set, then fork up and leave for 10 minutes at normal room temperature to see how it holds. These few minutes of caution may save you from disaster.

For simple aspics
1 envelope (1 Tb) gelatin for each 2 cups (½ L) consommé

For lining a mold
1 envelope (1 Tb) gelatin for each 1½ cups (3½ dL) consommé

Preserved Goose

Confit d'oie

In the old days before anyone had heard of refrigerators and freezers, and even before the invention of canning, you had to preserve meats in some manner to last you through the lean months. For meats, a typical method was first to salt them, then to cook them slowly in fat, and finally to put them down in fat. In French that process was known (and still is) as a *confit,* which comes from the Latin *conficere,* to digest— and that, in a way, is what salt does to meats and sugar to fruits; the fat holds the cooked food in hermetically sealed suspension. A *confit* is a primitive form of canning.

Why bother doing it nowadays, then, when we have modern preserving methods?

Well, it has a special character all its own, just as corned beef and sausages have their own special tastes. And, if you don't want to cook a whole goose, you can turn part of it into a ragout, and preserve the rest in a *confit.* Then, for people who love to cook it's fun and interesting to do, and a wonderful resource to have in one's refrigerator, since it is ever ready to furnish forth an unusually fine emergency meal.

Fat Note: This type of preserving sounds as though it would result in very fatty meat, but the contrary is true because the fat renders out of the goose skin as it cooks, and the goose meat, which is lean anyway, does not absorb the rendering fat. You can skin the goose after cooking, and dip each piece into hot broth or even hot water to dissolve and remove all of the clinging preserving fat. Goose fat, however, is a delicious commodity for use in frying potatoes, flavoring vegetables, basting meats, and it keeps for months in your refrigerator— or may be used again and again for preserving more geese, ducks, pork, and so forth and so on.

Clockwise from upper left: gizzard and carcass bits for broth, fat for rendering, liver and heart for pâtés; skin cracklings; cut-up goose pieces ready for confit; broth; the whole goose; the finished confit

For Salting the Goose—24 hours:
A 10- to 12-pound (4½- to 5½-kg) "roaster" goose
4 to 5 Tb coarse or kosher salt, sea salt, or regular salt
⅛ tsp saltpeter (from a pharmacy; optional)
⅛ tsp pepper and a big pinch each juniper berries, allspice, thyme, and bay leaf, all finely ground

For Rendering Fat and Cooking Goose:
6 to 8 cups (1½ to 2 L) fat—goose fat and fatty skin, plus fresh pork fat and/or lard (more if needed)
1 cup (¼ L) water

Equipment:
A large crock or heavy plastic bag to hold the goose pieces and something to weight them down during maceration; a large kettle or saucepan for rendering fat and cooking goose; frying thermometer for testing fat useful; a crock or bowl fitted with a rack for storing goose

Cutting up and salting goose
(24 hours)

Remove wings at elbows, and cut goose into drumstick, thigh, wing–lower breast, and breast-with-bone pieces; chop breast into three crosswise pieces. Chop up carcass, neck, and wings, and save for a stock (see page 61) or soup; heart and peeled gizzard can go into the

Weight down the goose pieces after salting.

confit, or into a stew (gizzard peel into soup); liver can be used like chicken liver.

Mix the salt, optional saltpeter (for preserving rosy color), and spices in a bowl; rub into all sides of goose. Pack goose pieces into crock and weight down with a plate and canned goods or other heavy objects; or pack into a bag, squeeze out air, and tie closed, then weight down in a bowl. Leave for 24 hours.

🕐 You may leave it a day or 2 longer—but if you want to keep it for several weeks, triple the salt and spices, and remember to soak the goose pieces overnight in cold water to remove excess salt before using.

Rendering the fat
About 1 hour

Meanwhile, cut fat and fatty skin pieces into rough slices and place in kettle over moderate heat; add the water and cover the kettle to let the fat liquefy and render out slowly—20 to 25 minutes. When it has rendered, skin pieces will begin to brown; watch fat temperature from now on. Fat must remain a clear yellow; temperature should not go over 325°F/165°C. When skin pieces are a light golden brown the fat has rendered; dip them out with a slotted spoon or sieve, and drain fat drippings back into kettle. (Save pieces and turn into cracklings; see end of recipe.)

🕐 Fat may be rendered in advance. When cool, cover and refrigerate.

Cooking the goose
About 1½ hours

When you are ready to cook the goose, rub off the salt with paper towels, and liquefy fat if it has cooled and congealed. Place goose in kettle

When skin pieces are lightly browned, fat has rendered.

with fat; goose pieces will swell slightly as they cook, and skin will render more fat, but the pieces should be covered by liquid fat at all times. Add lard, if necessary. Start timing when fat begins to bubble, and maintain temperature at 200 to 205°F/95 to 96°C. Goose is done when meat is tender if pierced with a sharp-pronged fork.

To preserve the goose
The goose is delicious, hot and just cooked, as is, or allowed to cool and eaten cold. To preserve, remove goose pieces from fat and arrange them in a crock, wide-mouthed jar, or bowl that has been fitted with a rack—goose pieces should not rest on the bottom because you want liquid fat to surround and protect them. (Dry twigs, bark removed, work perfectly well here instead of a rack.) Bring the cooking fat to the simmer and let cook until it stops spluttering—5 minutes or so—indicating any liquids have evaporated. Pour it through a strainer, lined with several thicknesses of cheesecloth, over the goose pieces. Shake crock gently to allow grease to flow throughout, and when goose is completely covered, let cool and congeal. Pour on more fat if any pieces protrude. Cover with plastic wrap and refrigerate.

🕐   The goose will keep at around 37°F/3°C for 3 to 4 months or longer.

Removing pieces of goose
To remove goose pieces, set container in a bowl of hot water until fat has softened, then remove as many pieces as you wish. Cover the rest completely with the fat, and store as before.

Meat shrinks from drumstick during cooking. You can remove bone if you wish.

Goose Fat:
Goose fat, as previously noted but it bears repeating, will keep for months in a covered jar in the refrigerator. Use it for sautéing potatoes, for basting roasts, for cooking such earthy items as cabbage, dried beans, turnips, or for cooking more *confit*.

Cracklings—Residue from the Rendering of Fat:
You may toss the bits of browned skin, left from fat rendering, in a sprinkling of salt, pepper, and allspice, and serve either as a cocktail snack or along with the cassoulet. Or chop them fine, warm briefly in a frying pan with the seasonings, pack into a jar, and cover with a thin layer of hot goose fat; seal top with plastic wrap and refrigerate—for use as a cocktail cracker spread (known in French as *frittons* or *grattons*).

Goose Stock:
To make a stock out of the chopped-up carcass, wings, neck, and gizzard peelings, place in a large saucepan with a peeled and quartered onion, a carrot, a small leek if you have one, and a celery stalk with leaves. Pour on cold water to cover ingredients by 2 inches (5 cm), salt lightly, and add an herb bouquet (6 parsley sprigs, 1 bay leaf, 1 garlic clove, 4 allspice berries, and ½ tsp thyme). Bring to the simmer, skim off gray scum, which will continue to rise for several minutes, then cover loosely and simmer 2½ hours, adding more water if liquid evaporates below level of ingredients. Strain, let cool, then refrigerate; remove congealed fat from surface when chilled. Use for soups and sauces, or combine with other stock for the consommé earlier in this chapter.

🕐   Will keep several days under refrigeration; may be frozen for several months.

Preserved Duck, Turkey, Pork, and Small Game Such as Squirrel and Rabbit:
Treat any of the above as you would goose, cutting the meat into serving pieces before salting it and simmering it in rendered pork fat or lard.

Cassoulet

Beans baked with lamb, goose, and sausages

For a 6-quart (6-L) casserole, serving 10 to 12 people

For the Beans:

To make 3 ½ quarts or 3 ¼ L cooked beans

5 cups (2 pounds or 900 g) dry white beans—Great Northern or small white

4 ½ quarts (4 L) water

1 pound (450 g) fat-and-lean salt pork with rind (optional)

1 large yellow onion, peeled and sliced

1 large herb bouquet (8 parsley sprigs, 4 cloves garlic, ½ tsp thyme, and 2 imported bay leaves, all tied in washed cheesecloth)

Salt as needed

For the Lamb:

About 4 pounds (2 kg) bone-in lamb shoulder, sawed into stewing chunks

Rendered goose fat, or cooking oil

2 large onions, sliced

4 or 5 large cloves garlic, minced

½ cup (1 dL) tomato sauce (page 111), or 4 or 5 Tb tomato paste

½ tsp thyme

2 imported bay leaves

2 cups (½ L) dry white wine or dry white French vermouth

3 cups (¾ L) or more beef stock or bouillon

Salt and pepper

Other Ingredients:

About ½ the preserved goose in the preceding recipe, and the cracklings

1 ½ to 2 pounds (675 to 900 g) cooking sausage such as kielbasy or chorizo, or sausage meat formed into cakes

3 Tb or more rendered goose fat or melted butter

2 cups (½ L) moderately pressed down, fresh white crumbs from crustless nonsweet French or Italian bread

½ cup (1 dL) moderately pressed down minced fresh parsley

Equipment:

An 8-quart (7- to 8-L) kettle or pressure cooker for the beans; a medium-sized casserole or chicken fryer for the lamb; a 6-quart (6-L) flameproof casserole for baking the cassoulet

The beans

Pick over the beans to be sure there are no stones or other debris among them, wash and drain them, and place in a large kettle or in the bottom of a large pressure cooker. Add the water, cover, and bring to the boil. Boil uncovered for exactly 2 minutes. Cover and let sit for exactly 1 hour. (This takes the place of the old-fashioned overnight soak.) Meanwhile, if you are using salt pork, remove the rind, and cut the pork into slices ½ inch (1½ cm) thick; simmer rind and pork in 3 quarts (3 L) water for 15 minutes to remove excess salt; rinse in cold water, drain, and set aside.

The braised lamb shoulder (a good dish just as is)

As soon as the beans have had their soak, bring to the simmer again, adding the optional pork and rind, the onion, the herb package, and 1 tablespoon salt if you have not used salt pork — ½ tablespoon if you have. Either simmer slowly, partially covered, for about 1½ hours or until the beans are just tender (add boiling water if needed, to keep beans covered at all times, and salt to taste near end of cooking). Or pressure cook as follows: cover and bring to full pressure for exactly 2 minutes; remove from heat and let pressure go down by itself for 15 minutes, then remove pressure knob; taste, and add salt as necessary.

🕐   The beans may be cooked 2 or 3 days in advance; when cool, cover and refrigerate. Bring just to the simmer before proceeding with the cassoulet.

The lamb — braised shoulder of lamb

Dry the lamb pieces. Film casserole or chicken fryer with fat or oil, heat to very hot but not smoking, and brown the lamb pieces, a few at a time, removing those that are browned to a side dish. Pour out excess fat, and brown the onions lightly. Then return all lamb to casserole, add the garlic, tomato, herbs, and wine or vermouth, and enough stock or bouillon just to cover the lamb. Salt lightly to taste, cover, and simmer slowly for about 1½ hours, or until lamb is tender. Carefully correct seasoning; when cool, remove and discard bones from lamb.

🕐   May be cooked several days in advance; when cold, cover and refrigerate the lamb in its cooking liquid. Discard congealed surface fat before using.

Assembling the cassoulet

Remove bones from preserved goose and, if you wish, the skin; cut goose into serving chunks about the same size as your lamb pieces. If you are using salt pork, cut it into thin slices. If you are using sausage such as kielbasy, cut in half lengthwise, then into chunks, and brown lightly in a frying pan with goose fat or oil. If you are using sausage meat, form into cakes about 1 ½ inches (4 cm) across, and brown in fat or oil.

With a slotted spoon, dip beans from their liquid (be sure to save it) and arrange about ⅓ of them in the bottom of the casserole you have chosen for the cassoulet. Cover with a layer of lamb, goose, sausage, a handful of goose cracklings, and, if you are using it, half the salt pork. Repeat with a layer of beans and of meat; end with a layer of beans, coming to within about ¼ inch (¾ cm) of the rim of the casserole. Ladle on the lamb-cooking liquid plus as much bean-cooking liquid as needed just to cover the beans. Spread bread crumbs and parsley over the top.

🕐 May be assembled a day or even 2 days in advance, but if the beans and lamb have not been freshly cooked, be sure to bring them to the simmer for several minutes before assembling, to prevent any possibility of spoilage. When cool, cover and refrigerate.

1) Cutting the sausages before browning

2) A layer of beans goes in.

3) Spooning liquid over top

4) Breaking the crust into the beans

Warning on refrigerated cassoulets

The assembled cassoulet needs a good hour of baking so that all elements can combine deliciously together, thus the contents of the casserole must be decongealed and simmering before the actual baking effect can begin. Heating on top of the stove can be risky because you may scorch the bottom of the beans. I suggest, then, that the casserole be covered and set in a 325°F/165°C oven for an hour or so until its contents are bubbling; test center with a thermometer if you have any doubts—it should read 212°F/100°C. Then proceed with the baking in the next step. (I have had my troubles in this category, thinking that, because things were bubbling in the oven, the cassoulet was baking properly when it was just cooking around the edges but had not really heated through.)

Baking

About 1 hour

Preheat oven to 400°F/205°C. Bring casserole to simmer on top of the stove (or see preceding paragraph if casserole has been refrigerated), then set in oven. Bake for 20 to 30 minutes, until bread crumb topping has crusted and browned lightly; break the crust into the beans with the back of a spoon, and return the casserole to the oven. Lower thermostat to 350°F/180°C, and continue baking for another 15 minutes or so, until a second crust has formed itself on top. Break it, in turn, into the beans, and if cooking liquid seems too thick or the beans dry, add a spoonful or so of bean-cooking liquid from your pot. When the crust forms again, leave it as is; the beans are ready to serve.

❶   The beans will stay warm in a turned-off oven, door ajar, for a good half hour, or you may keep them warm on an electric hot tray. They will gradually dry out if kept too warm for too long a time.

Pickled Red Cabbage Slaw

You can't treat red cabbage like green cabbage, I have found, at least if you want to serve it raw. It needs to be very finely shredded and wants a maceration of a day or 2 in a solution of salt and vinegar to tenderize it; being a red vegetable, it must have some acid with it anyway to keep its color. The following is, I think, a refreshing way to serve it, being neither too sharp nor too picklelike, and a fine accompaniment to the likes of a cassoulet.

For about 2 quarts (2 L)

A good fresh red cabbage weighing about 1½ pounds (675 g)

A large red onion

A large sweet red bell pepper (optional)

2 to 3 cloves garlic, minced

4 imported bay leaves

1 tsp mustard seeds

½ tsp juniper berries

½ cup (1 dL) canned beet juice, or borscht

1 cup (¼ L) red wine vinegar (more if needed)

The sweet-and-sour charm of pickled red cabbage slaw

| 2 cups (½ L) water (more if needed) |
| 2 Tb salt (more if needed) |
| 1 Tb sugar |
| 4 tart apples |
| 4 handfuls minced fresh parsley |

| Equipment: |
| A cabbage shredder, such as a mail-order sauerkraut cutter, or other device, or an expert person with a very sharp stainless-steel knife (carbon steel can turn the cabbage blue) |

Discard wilted outer leaves, halve and quarter the cabbage, and cut out the core. Cut cabbage into shreds as thin and fine as possible—$^1/_{16}$ inch (¼ cm); do the same with the onion and optional pepper. The finer and thinner you cut the vegetables, the more efficiently the flavors can penetrate and tenderize the cabbage and the more successful your relish. Toss in a bowl with the garlic, bay, mustard, juniper, and beet juice or borscht. Bring the vinegar and water to the simmer with the salt and sugar, pour over the cabbage, and toss to mix well. Pack into a 2-quart (2-L) jar. Liquid should just cover ingredients by a finger width—add more vinegar and water in the proportions of 1 part vinegar to 2 parts water if necessary. Cover and refrigerate, turning jar upside down several times for the first 2 days; taste, and add a little more salt if you feel it necessary. The relish should marinate for 2 days at least.

When ready to serve, dip out as much of the relish as you think you will need, and for every 2 cups (½ L), blend in 1 minced apple and a handful of parsley.

❶ The cabbage will keep for at least several weeks under refrigeration, and the pickling juice may be used over and over again—just add more seasoning if you think it is needed.

Sliced Fresh Pineapple— En Boat

In its shell

For 10 to 12 people

| 2 of the largest, ripest, sweetest, and finest pineapples available (or 3 or even 4 smaller pineapples; see Remarks, page 57) |
| Sprigs of fresh mint, if available |
| White rum or kirsch (optional) |

| Equipment: |
| A very sharp, long heavy knife for slicing the whole pineapple; a smaller very sharp flexible knife for other cutting; a platter upon which to serve the pineapple |

Cutting and Slicing Note:
While trying things out for the television show depicting this dinner, all of us cooks had a hand in cutting pineapples. We used the coring gadget. We tried a long knife. We shaved off the peel all around and spiraled the eyes out of a pineapple. And we even butchered another pineapple trying a half-remembered system of somebody's grandmother, who, it was said, cut diamond wedges around each eye, slanting into the pineapple so each wedge could be pulled out individually—the pineapple collapsed halfway through. We all preferred the following.

Cut the pineapple in half, being very careful when you come to the crown to keep it attached to the fruit—for decoration later. Then cut the halves into lengthwise halves or thirds. Cut out the hard core at the top of each wedge; with a sharp flexible knife, cut close against the skin to free the wedge of flesh. Then, if the wedge seems a bit wide, cut it in half lengthwise before cutting it crosswise into wedge-shaped slices. Replace the slices on the skin—or boat—and arrange attractively on a platter with, if you wish, sprigs of fresh mint.

🕐   If not to be served promptly, cover closely with plastic wrap and refrigerate.

As you serve the pineapple at the table, and particularly if it is not as sweet as you could wish, you might drizzle a few drops of rum or kirsch over each wedge.

Cut against skin to release pineapple wedges; at the table drizzle on rum or kirsch.

🕐 *Timing*

Last-minute planning won't work for a cassoulet party, obviously, but the nice thing is that there are practically no last-minute *jobs* with this menu.

Half an hour before sitting down, put the cracker bread in the oven to crisp for 5 minutes (careful it doesn't scorch), set the consommé on the stove ready to heat, and check the cassoulet. If it is done, turn off the oven.

Whether it should be 1½ hours or 3 hours before you intend to serve the cassoulet that you put it in the oven depends on whether or not it was made ahead and refrigerated. Since how long it simmers is crucial to its final flavor, please see the discussion of that important matter in the recipe itself, page 66.

Sometime in the afternoon, or even that morning, cut and refrigerate the pineapple, closely covered with plastic wrap.

The day before your party, or even the day before that, assemble the cassoulet. That same day, buy the pineapples, and maybe some parsley to garnish the red cabbage.

The day before *that*, in other words up to three days before your party, cook the lamb and the beans, and make and cook the sausage if you're doing your own. (There's a good recipe for homemade sausage meat on page 110.) You could preserve the goose now, if you had thought to buy and defrost your bird 2 or 3 days beforehand; then you could cook the *confit* while you were braising the lamb—the goose needs a 24-hour salting before it cooks, however. But you can cook a *confit* months ahead and "put it down"—that's the point of it anyway, to have something marvelous and waiting.

As much as 2 weeks beforehand, you can pickle the red cabbage, but it does need its jar tipped once or twice for the first 2 days.

Clarify the consommé any time at all, and keep it in the freezer.

Menu Variations

If you weren't having a fruit dessert, you could move your pineapples up front and, rather than consommé, serve them sliced with prosciutto, or use some other fruit for your *first course*. I love a plain chilled half grapefruit or melon—a perfect specimen. Just be sure you have something light before cassoulet; shellfish seem to me too bland and too meaty, somehow. You want piquancy.

The *cassoulet* can be infinitely varied. Bearing in mind that the dish was not conceived in a fancy restaurant with bought-to-order ingredients, do experiment with whatever you have on hand. Some of your combinations will, of course, be better than others, and some you may decide never to try again. You can use sausages only, or roast or braised pork instead of lamb, or duck or turkey instead of (or along with) goose, or ham hocks or veal shanks, or such small game as squirrel or rabbit. You can use other kinds of dry beans, or lentils, or even fresh beans. I've never tried limas or Kentucky Wonders, but you might. One item you must have, however, is a good cooking stock of some sort to pour over the beans and give them real flavor during their final baking. As for a vegetarian cassoulet, how about lots and lots of garlic, onions, tomatoes, herbs, and perhaps the sautéed eggplant on page 78?

Not too many accompaniments occur to me as good substitutes for the *pickled red cabbage*. Sauerkraut is a possibility, or coleslaw, or you might like a chiffonade salad—lettuce with sliced cooked (preferably pickled) beets and a light sieving of hard-boiled egg, for that sweet-sour taste. Or you could try sliced cucumbers, lightly wilted with salt, then drained well, tossed in a little lemon juice with a few grains of sugar and some finely chopped red onion, and sprinkled with parsley.

For *dessert*, pineapple does seem ideal to me; but you could serve ice-cold very ripe persimmons, Persian or honeydew melon, or sliced oranges, plain or with blueberries, or perhaps glazed, as in *Mastering I,* or perhaps a sherbet.

If you had a first course of fruit, a coffee granita (the large-crystal sherbet) might be nice. Here's a last-minute trick we tried and liked after one cassoulet dinner: if you have a food processor, use the steel blade and dump in frozen sliced peaches cut in chunks plus ⅓ their volume of Champagne and drops of lemon juice; process, sugar to taste, and process again. The whole thing takes two minutes and gives you a sherbet of perfect ready-to-eat consistency.

Leftovers

A fully cooked *cassoulet* can be reheated and is very good, but usually not quite as good as after its first baking. Be sure it is moist enough; add a little stock if it's not. Or you can turn the remains into a soup: mince the meats (slicing the sausage) and add them to the beans, puréed in stock.

When you have made your own *preserved goose*, you have a splendid kitchen staple on hand, in fact several. The *fat* can be re-used many times, if you don't overheat it, and is delicious for preserving other meats, or for frying. The *goose stock*, like any stock, can become a consommé or can go into soups, sauces, and stews, and can of course be frozen. If you have *cracklings* to spare, you can treat them as suggested earlier in the chapter and use as a cocktail cracker spread. The preserved meat is delicious cold: dip the pieces in boiling stock or even boiling water to remove fat, and you may also wish to discard the skin. Season lightly and roll in a mixture of finely chopped parsley and shallots. Serve with potato salad, watercress, or curly endive with a garlic and bacon dressing, or with a hearty mixed vegetable salad. If you're having a pot of beans, lentils, sauerkraut, braised cabbage, or the like, you can bury the goose pieces in the beans or cabbage and let them warm up for 8 to 10 minutes before serving. Or you can add pieces of preserved goose to a boiled dinner or *pot-au-feu*, giving them 4 to 5 minutes to simmer with the meats, just before serving. (They do get stringy if overcooked, so be careful.) Or you can roll the goose pieces in seasoned bread crumbs, baste with droplets of goose fat, and let warm under a slow broiler for 4 to 5 minutes on each side, or until hot through and tender. Serve with a purée of turnips, potatoes, parsnips, dried beans or lentils, or braised onions, celery, or leeks, or with sauerkraut or braised cabbage, or with Brussels sprouts or broccoli.

The *pickled cabbage* will keep for weeks in the refrigerator, and may be used hot as well as cold; wouldn't it be nice in a sizzling Reuben sandwich? And you can re-use the pickling juice when you run out of cabbage.

Pineapple doesn't keep long. You can serve leftover bits the next day with other cut-up fruit (strawberries especially), or use it instead of crackers with cream cheese and guava jelly or Bar-le-Duc preserve. With slices of prosciutto, it makes a sublime first course, and dieters, as we all know, mix it with their penitential low-fat cottage cheese. But don't try freezing it or putting it in an aspic: no go.

Postscript: They're funny that way

Cassoulet de Castelnaudary, Cassoulet de Toulouse, Cassoulet de Carcassonne . . . they're all good, and so's the cassoulet I've just described. So too are any number of variants. For most of us, which cassoulet we make or concoct depends on what looks good in the market. For the peasant cooks who probably thought up the dish in the first place, it most certainly depended on what was available. Fresh meat would have been used if an animal had just been slaughtered; otherwise, before the invention of refrigeration, every Mrs. French Peasant had to rely on what she had preserved. If she raised geese for a cash crop of *foie gras,* using only the livers, then *confit d'oie* would take care of the liverless gaggle. At hog-killing time, salting and the making of "summer" (keeping) sausage would preserve any meat not eaten fresh. From *confit d'oie,* she could progress to *confit de canard* if she raised ducks. Dry beans keep and they, like other legumes good for cassoulet, can be grown almost anywhere.

Certainly cassoulet's earthy simplicity, its lack of expensive or exotic ingredients, its nourishing heartiness suggest a peasant origin. Because an oven was something of a luxury in the poorer farmhouses of France, country women always used to carry their pots to the village baker, to be placed in his still-hot oven when the morning's last batch of bread was done.

Only history locates cassoulet in Languedoc, since the ingredients are easily produced almost anywhere in France. But that doesn't prevent French gastronomes from endlessly rehashing often unsubstantiated legends about the veritable cassoulet, and quarreling fervently over which of three towns—all quite close by—produced the truest and best, the one and only, cassoulet.

And yet I wonder: why *are* the French so passionate, not just about food itself or about naming dishes for their authentic region of origin (like potatoes *à la dauphinoise,* or our New England baked beans)—but for naming them after tiny, insignificant localities? We Americans have a few dishes named for big cities, and the English have a few named for counties (Devonshire cream, Cornish pasties, Yorkshire pudding, etc.), but nothing like this intense particularity. Doesn't the brouhaha over names and attributions arise from an almost amorous sense of place, a lover's appreciation of the special character of every corner of the land? For it's not just cassoulet the French are geographically potty about, it's bouillabaisse and pâté and all kinds of things to eat. Why they and not other great cooks like the Chinese?

There is, though, another nation of great cooks, the Italians, who are similarly inclined, with their myriad dishes *alla* somewhere-*ese*. The scholar Mario Pei has said that's because Italy was broken up until so recently into tiny city-states, each with its own cuisine. Not so true of France.

But almost every little place in both France and Italy makes its own particular wine, and it is part of wine's magic to speak with eloquence and precision of the very earth it came from. Grow the same grapes by similar methods in vineyards yards apart, and you often get unlike wines. How natural, then, for the children of wine-making cultures to be so sensitive to the special personality of every field and hill. How natural for them to name a garnish of peas for Clamart, an otherwise dull place that grows fine peas, or one of spinach for little Viroflay, or to name variants, as with

cassoulet, for the places where they are supposed to have been invented.

For a Frenchman, a mental map of France must look like a vast hexagonal buffet. Even for me, some dishes powerfully evoke a beloved region. When I taste an apple tart *à la normande,* all fresh and creamy, my mind's eye dwells on the drowsy cattle and the scented orchards Paul and I drove past en route to Paris from the war-shattered docks of Cherbourg, on my first day in France thirty-odd years ago. And where is my mind's eye now, as I taste this excellent cassoulet? Why, on the busy kitchen behind the *J.C. & Co.* set, where we of the cooking team developed our own version. Above us looms not the sunny sky of fabled Languedoc, but a frightful mess of pipes and lights and rubber-covered cables. Nevertheless, this too is a beloved place. Ought we, perhaps, to name our dish in the classic fashion *Cassoulet des Coulisses de J.C. et Cie.,* or J.C. & Co.'s Backstage Cassoulet?

A delightful meal for epicures of almost any dietary persuasion

A Vegetarian Caper

Menu
For 6 people

Spaghetti Squash Tossed with Eggplant Persillade

❧

Gâteau of Crêpes—Layered with vegetables and cheese

❧

Mixed Green Salad
Hot French Bread

❧

Ice Cream and a Rum and Meatless Mincemeat Sauce

❧

Suggested wines:
A light red wine like a Bordeaux, Beaujolais, or merlot; or a rosé; or a dry riesling or Chablis

"That was *so* good!" a friend exclaimed the other day. "Maybe I'll change my ways, too!" It took me a minute to catch on: she thought Paul and I had become vegetarians because we'd just served a dinner without meat, fish, or fowl. (And why not? There's no law . . .) No, we're not about to change our ways, which are omnivorous; but our pace, certainly. Any time. And this was one of those mild late-winter days when melting snow trills in the gutters and you hear birds and smell the earth again. Suddenly we craved light food and fresh flavors, and this menu hit the spot.

We serve it to carnivores, but it was, I admit, designed originally for vegetarian friends who happen to be of the moderate, or ovo-lacto, persuasion, meaning that they use eggs and milk and cheese. On the whole, I think the soft full flavors of dairy items are the ideal enrichment for good fresh produce; indeed, this sort of cooking is a stimulus to me. I would, though, find it a bit dull to work for long within the restrictions set by purist vegetarians.

Marcella Hazan, that queen of Italian cookery, presented me with my first spaghetti squash a few years ago, and it turns out that they are easily grown almost everywhere. We're seeing more and more of them in the markets, and a fine thing that is. You steam your great golden whopper whole, halve it and seed it, and then, heaven knows why, the flesh turns into spaghetti right under the spoon as you scoop it onto the platter: fine, long, bright-gold strands with a crunchy juicy texture. Like spaghetti, its flavor is bland, so that it takes beautifully to sauces and garnishes: all the exuberance of pasta without the concomitant calories! For this menu, and a hearty main dish to come, we use eggplant tossed with parsley and garlic (in itself a good dish); in the recipe I've suggested a nice variant as well, using sesame seeds. (If this meal weren't so strong in protein — I calculate that it affords one almost a full day's supply — sesame seeds would be a good way to boost it. Like mushrooms, they're prized by vegetarians for this reason. I like them simply because they are delicious.)

A stratum of practicality underlies the charm and the festive air of concerned hosts, and the same could be said of our main dish. Not only can it be largely prepared in advance,

but it's good hot or cold, and is so compact and easily served that we often take it along (in its mold, of course) on fork picnics. You can use any combination of vegetables to fill the crêpe-walled compartments. As for crêpes themselves, they're one of the most versatile elements in cookery, one of the first things a beginning cook should master. Only their name poses a problem.

For the tomato sauce recipe, don't look in this chapter but in the Appendix in the back of this book, where I've grouped a few basics. This is a sauce I use to add piquant flavor and brilliant color to all kinds of dishes: it has accompanied a boiled dinner, lasagne, and a baked fish with equal success, which gives you an idea of its versatility; you might also like to try it with an omelet sometime, or with a soufflé. The gâteau doesn't need a sauce, having plenty of flavor on its own, but enhancement is the name of the game in cooking an all-veg meal, and I like the look of the stratified slice in a sparkling red puddle. (In general, I prefer the old-fashioned custom of saucing around, not over, food.)

One recipe I am sorry *not* to supply here is one for homemade French bread. I've given it twice before, in *Mastering II* and in *J.C.'s Kitchen,* and it just takes too much space. It's not that a long recipe means a long job; with practice, most cooks find it takes about 15 minutes' working time per batch. The quality is seraphic, and I hope you'll want to try it. As for green salad, look in Appendix again for a basic vinaigrette dressing, vary it to your taste, and choose the freshest greens in the grocery.

Marvelously inquisitive and resourceful, the really good cooks among my vegetarian friends have steered me toward many good things to eat. I have vast respect for their imagination and care in cooking, and for the way they seek out the ultimate in fresh, exquisite produce. And for their realism and, well, sense of proportion. In America we still eat needless, indeed preposterous, quantities of animal protein, but I think the time is coming when we'll have to join with the rest of the world.

Preparations and Marketing

Recommended Equipment:
If you don't have a big kettle or covered roaster, and a steaming rack, you can bake the spaghetti squash in the oven.

The gâteau recipe precisely fills a 2-quart (2-L) dish. I use the French charlotte mold 3½ inches (9 cm) deep, the one I like for soufflés, since it produces a dramatically tall Hadrian's Tomb–type cylinder; but any straight-sided, deep, ovenproof dish will do. When it's done, the gâteau will let you know by puffing up and becoming divinely fragrant, but you can make a more precise test by using an instant, microwave type of thermometer, a gadget you'll use for meats, poultry, and all kinds of other dishes as well.

For crêpes, while it's nice to have the classic French pan, a shallow iron one about 6 inches (15 cm) in diameter, with an angled handle for easy flipping will do; I also like an American-made one of thick cast aluminum with a nonstick lining. Because crêpe batter is very runny, you must have a pan the size you want your crêpe to be. That rules out pancake griddles and big frying pans, but not those amusing patented devices that make crêpes upside down or right side up.

Staples to Have on Hand:

Salt
Peppercorns
Nutmeg
Optional: fresh or fragrant dried dill weed
Optional: saffron threads
Optional: dried orange peel
Imported bay leaves
Italian or Provençal herb mixture
Olive oil ▼
Butter
Optional: fresh sesame or peanut oil
Flour: Wondra or instant-blending type
    preferred ▼
Milk
Optional: heavy cream (1 cup or ¼ L)
Garlic
Shallots or scallions
Lemons (1)
Optional: canned Italian plum tomatoes
Dark Jamaica rum or bourbon whiskey

Specific Ingredients for This Menu:

Swiss cheese (½ pound or 225 g)
Cream cheese (½ pound or 225 g) ▼
Eggs (9 "large")
Optional: Parmesan cheese (½ pound or 225 g)
Salad greens
Parsley
Onions (2 medium)
Broccoli (1 bunch) ▼
Carrots (1 pound or 450 g) ▼
Eggplant (1 large) ▼
Spaghetti squash (1 large) ▼
Tomatoes (9 or 10 large) ▼
Mushrooms (1 pound or 450 g) ▼
French bread
Vanilla ice cream (1½ quarts or 1½ L)
Meatless mincemeat (1 jar)

▶ ## Remarks:
Staples to have on hand

Olive oil: if you want the best quality and are willing to pay for it, see that it is labeled "virgin olive oil," which means that this was the first pressing of the olives and that they were pressed cold. Olives are pressed not once but several times, and in later batches, in order to extract more oil, they are usually warmed. Be sure in any case that the label reads "pure olive oil," since otherwise it may contain adulterants. On keeping olive oil, there are many and fervent controversies—whether to decant it, whether it should breathe, etc.—but I have never had any trouble keeping an opened half gallon of olive oil, covered and stored in a cool dark closet. *Flour:* Wondra, or other instant-blending type, is good for crêpes, since it mixes smoothly and almost instantly in cold liquid, and you don't have to let your batter rest an hour or two before using it, as you would with regular flour.

Specific ingredients for this menu
(With special thanks to *Crockett's Victory Garden* and to *Wyman's Gardening Encyclopedia*)

Cream cheese: best of all is the fresh kind, without gluey additives and preservatives, but it will keep only 3 days or so in the refrigerator. *Broccoli:* it's passé if the florets have begun to open. Ideal stalk length, below where the stem branches, is from 4 to 6 inches (10 to 15 cm); if the base of the stem is hollow, cut that part off, since it will be tough. *Carrots:* buy firm crisp carrots, refrigerate them in a plastic bag, and use them soon. *Eggplant:* take pains; you can turn people off this lovely vegetable for life by serving a bad one. Buy shiny, firm, taut-skinned ones, use them within 2 or 3 days, and do not keep them too cold. Soft spots and the slightest sign of wrinkle or shrivel or flab are all bad news. Although they are picked when the seeds are still sparse, soft, and immature, eggplants vary greatly in shape and in size—from 6-inch (15-cm) midgets to foot-long monsters. Most of those in your market will be the deep-purple variety, but ivory, green, and mottled purple types exist and are similarly cooked. *Mushrooms:* the cultivated ones are best when the caps are curled tight to the stem, so that you can't see the gills. Refrigerate in a plastic bag and use as soon as you can, before they darken or soften. For field mushrooms, pick none you can't positively identify as edible. Dr. Wyman recommends Alexander H. Smith's *The Mushroom Hunter's Field Guide* (Ann Arbor: University of Michigan Press, revised edition, 1969). A standard field guide used by many mycologists I know is *One Thousand American Fungi,* by Charles McIlvaine and Robert K. Macadam (New York: Dover Publications, 1973), and one of my favorites for recipes is Jane Grigson's *The Mushroom Feast* (New York: Alfred A. Knopf, 1975, now in The Lyons Press paperback edition). *Spaghetti squash:* use the fingernail test to be sure the rind is soft; if hard, the squash was picked when too mature.

Eggplant and spaghetti squash

Here's a puzzle: the grower I consulted says its botanical name is *Cucurbita ficifolia,* and that it is a gourd of tropical origin. All the ones I've seen are bright gold, but a delightful old book by Cora, Rose, and Bob Brown, *The Vegetable Cook Book: From Trowel to Table* (Philadelphia: J. B. Lippincott, 1939), says it's cream-white like a honeydew melon. You can tell at a glance that it's a cucurbit, like cucumbers, squash, gourds, pumpkins, and some melons; but the great horticultural authority Dr. Wyman gives the name *C. ficifolia* to a white, *in*edible fruit (or vegetable) grown in the tropics and commonly called Malabar gourd. His encyclopedia doesn't describe anything like my big beauty. *Tomatoes:* the U.S. Department of Agriculture says so, county agents say so, any farmer who knows a hoe from a harrow says so, and I'm so sick of saying so that now I sing it instead. In my sleep. But the markets still plod along with their thumbs in their ears and their minds in neutral. What do we tomato lovers have to do, for pity's sake? Well, again: in the summertime, you can buy locally grown tomatoes that are ripe or that will ripen. However, no tomato at any season will ever ripen if it has been kept at a temperature of less than 40 °F/4.5 °C for any length of time; it may eventually turn red, but its flavor-developing facilities have been killed. In fact, any temperature less than 50 °F/10 °C is bad news for the tomato. Even a picked green tomato that is old enough to have developed the normal amount of seeds and jelly in its interstices will ripen in a few days at room temperature—in a week or so if kept around 60 °F/16 °C—if it was never abused by a low temperature. Tomatoes should never ever be refrigerated unless they are so ripe they will spoil! Any market that stores an unripened tomato in a refrigerated case has no sense of decency, no respect for tomatoes, and certainly no knowledge at all about them —or concern for us, the tomato-buying public. (End of tomato discussion—for this book, anyway.)

Spaghetti Squash Tossed with Eggplant Persillade

Serving 6 people

1 spaghetti squash about 10 by 7 inches (25 by 18 cm)

1 eggplant about 9 by 5 inches (23 by 13 cm)

Salt and pepper

4 or more Tb olive oil

2 or more large cloves garlic, minced

5 to 6 Tb minced fresh parsley (a small bunch)

2 to 3 Tb butter (optional)

1 cup (¼ L) freshly grated Parmesan cheese (optional)

Equipment:

A kettle large enough to hold the squash, and a vegetable steaming rack (or you may boil or bake the squash); 1 or 2 large frying pans, nonstick recommended; a long-handled spoon and fork for table tossing

Preliminary cooking of spaghetti squash
To cook the squash, you may bake it for 1½ hours in a 350 °F/180 °C oven, or boil it for 20 to 30 minutes, or steam it. I opt for steaming, as the easiest method. Place a rack or colander in the bottom of a large kettle or roaster with a tight-fitting lid, add 1½ inches (4 cm) water, lay in the squash, and bring to the boil. (Weight down the lid if necessary, so the steam can do its work.) Steam for 25 to 30 minutes, or just until the outside of the squash will cede to the pressure of your fingers. Cut the squash open lengthwise, and scrape out the thick yellowish threads and big seeds from the center, going crosswise with a big spoon—careful here or you will mix these nonspaghetti threads with the real meat of the squash. Then scrape down the squash lengthwise, and the meat will separate itself into strands.

🕐   May be cooked and scraped even a day in advance; cover the spaghetti and refrigerate.

The Eggplant Persillade—Eggplant with Garlic and Parsley:
Having chosen a fine, firm, shiny eggplant, cut off the green cap, and remove the skin with a vegetable peeler. Cut into ½-inch (1½-cm) slices, cut the slices into ½-inch strips, and the strips into ½-inch dice. Toss

in a colander with ½ teaspoon salt, and let drain for at least 20 minutes, then dry in a towel. Film a large frying pan (preferably a nonstick one) with ⅛ inch (½ cm) olive oil, and sauté the eggplant over moderately high heat for 4 to 5 minutes, tossing frequently, until tender—test by tasting a piece. Add the garlic and toss for a minute to cook it, then toss with the parsley only at the last moment. Incidentally, this is a good dish all by itself, either hot or cold.

🕐 The eggplant may be cooked several hours in advance and set aside in a bowl, but do not add the parsley or reheat until the last moment.

Final assembly and serving
Heat several tablespoons of oil and/or butter in a large frying pan, add the spaghetti squash strands, tossing and turning over moderately high heat for several minutes to cook the squash a little more—or to your taste. Toss with salt and pepper, then turn out onto a hot platter. Spoon the hot eggplant in the center, and bring to the table. Then toss the spaghetti and eggplant together with, if you like, spoonfuls of cheese, and pass more cheese separately for those who wish it.

Variation:
Here is another squash and eggplant combination we like very much.

For the squash
Steam and shred the spaghetti squash as usual. Heat several tablespoons of oil in a large frying pan and swirl in 2 or 3 cloves of garlic, minced, cooking them gently for a minute or two. Then toss in the spaghetti squash and fold with the garlic, and salt and pepper to taste, adding more oil (or butter, if you wish) and cooking to the degree you prefer. Then toss with spoonfuls of Parmesan cheese, turn onto a hot platter, and garnish with the following eggplant. Serve the spaghetti squash with a piece or two of the eggplant—but do not toss them together.

Sesame baked eggplant
For one fine, firm, shiny eggplant about 9 inches long and 4 inches in diameter (23 by 10 cm). Cut the green top off the eggplant, and slice the eggplant into lengthwise quarters (or sixths), and each quarter (or sixth) into halves. Salt the flesh sides lightly and let stand 10 to 15 minutes, then pat dry with paper towels. Brush lightly on all sides with olive oil, and arrange skin side down in a shallow baking dish or jelly-roll pan. Bake in the upper third of a 425°F/220°C oven for about 15 minutes, or until the eggplant is soft. Meanwhile, toss ½ cup (1 dL) sesame seeds in a frying pan over moderate heat, shaking pan continuously until nicely toasted (they burn easily). Roll the cooked eggplant in the sesame seeds just before serving.

The squash turns into spaghetti as you scrape it out.

Gâteau of Crêpes

Molded mountain of crêpes layered with vegetables and cheese

Here is a handsome dish indeed, layers of fresh vegetables bound with a cheese custard, baked in a mold lined with crêpes—those multipurpose thin French pancakes. Serve it hot as a first course, a luncheon dish, or as the main course for a vegetarian meal, and any leftovers are good cold.

Serving 6 to 8 people

For the Crêpe Batter:

For 18 to 20 crêpes 5 ½ inches (14 cm) in diameter

1 cup (140 g) flour (Wondra or instant-blending preferred)

⅔ cup (1 ½ dL) each milk and water

3 "large" eggs

¼ tsp salt

3 Tb melted butter, or sesame or peanut oil

Vegetables and Cheese for Filling:

1 pound (450 g) carrots

6 to 8 Tb butter

Salt and pepper

½ tsp or so fresh or dried dill weed (optional)

1 pound (450 g) fresh mushrooms

4 Tb minced shallots or scallions

1 bunch (18 to 20 ounces or 500 to 550 g) fresh broccoli

2 cups (½ L) coarsely grated Swiss cheese

Custard Mixture for Filling:

1 cup (½ pound or 225 g) cream cheese

6 "large" eggs

1 cup (¼ L) milk and/or heavy cream

Salt and pepper

A pinch of nutmeg, to taste

Optional Sauce for the Gâteau:

2 ½ to 3 cups (about ¾ L) fresh tomato sauce (page 111; optional)

The gâteau cuts easily because the custard has set the layers.

Equipment:

A heavy cast-iron or cast-aluminum (nonstick recommended) frying pan with 5½-inch (14-cm) bottom diameter, for the crêpes; an 8-cup (2-L) baking dish, such as a metal charlotte mold, 4 inches (10 cm) deep; an instant (microwave) meat thermometer is recommended.

The crêpes—batter

Scoop dry-measure cup into flour container until cup is overflowing; sweep off excess with the straight edge of a knife, and pour flour into a pitcher or bowl. Blend the milk and water into the flour, beating with a whip until smooth (easy with Wondra or instant-blending flour), then beat in the eggs, salt, and butter or oil. Let rest for 10 minutes (an hour or 2 if you are using regular flour) so that flour granules can absorb the liquid—making a tender crêpe.

The crêpes—cooking

To cook the crêpes, heat frying pan or pans until drops of water sizzle on the surface. Brush lightly with a little butter (usually only necessary for the first crêpe), and pour 2 to 3 tablespoons or so of the batter into the center of the pan, turning the pan in all directions as you do so to spread the batter over the bottom surface. (If you have poured in too much, pour excess back into your batter bowl.) Cook for 30 seconds or so, until you see, when you lift an edge, that it is nicely browned. Turn and cook for 10 to 15 seconds more—this second

side never cooks evenly and is kept as the non-public or bottom side of the crêpe. Arrange crêpes, as they are made, on a cake rack so they will cool and dry off for 5 minutes or so. When dry (but not brittle!), stack together, wrap in foil, and place in a plastic bag.

🕐 Crêpes will keep for 2 to 3 days in the refrigerator. To freeze, it is best to package them in stacks of 6 or 8; either thaw at room temperature, or unpackage and heat in a covered dish in a moderate oven for 5 minutes or until they separate easily.

Note: I used to stack my cooked crêpes between sheets of wax paper or foil, but now that I have learned the cool-and-dry system, I have not found it necessary, even for freezing.

Preparing the vegetables

Trim and peel the carrots, and cut into julienne matchsticks. Sauté in 1½ tablespoons butter in a large frying pan, swirling and tossing frequently until carrots are nicely tender and being careful not to brown them. Season well with salt, pepper, and optional dill; set aside in a bowl.

Trim and wash the mushrooms, and cut into fine mince (a food processor is useful here); a handful at a time, twist the mushrooms in the corner of a clean towel to extract as much of their juice as possible. Sauté in the same large frying pan in 1½ tablespoons butter with the shallots or scallions, until the mushroom pieces begin to separate from each other. Season to taste with salt and pepper, and set aside in a separate bowl. This is now officially a mushroom *duxelles*.

Turning the crêpe to brown on the other side

Trim and wash the broccoli. Cut bud ends off stalks, to make them about 2 inches (5 cm) long. Starting at the cut ends, peel as much skin off as you easily can; peel skin off stalks, cutting down to expose tender whitish flesh, then cut into pieces half the length of your little finger—all this for quick and even cooking. Drop the peeled broccoli into 4 quarts (4 L) rapidly boiling salted water and boil uncovered for 3 to 5 minutes, or until just barely tender. Drain immediately; chop into pieces about ¼ inch (¾ cm) in size. Toss briefly in 2 tablespoons hot butter, and salt and pepper to taste. Set aside.

🕐   Carrots may be cooked a day ahead, and so may the broccoli; cover and refrigerate. Mushrooms may be cooked weeks ahead and stored in the freezer; be sure to defrost before using.

The custard mixture

To blend the cream cheese with the rest of the custard ingredients, either force it through a sieve with the eggs into a bowl and beat thoroughly, adding the rest of the ingredients, or mix everything together smoothly in a blender or food processor.

Assembling

Preheat oven to 350 °F/180 °C. Smear some butter over inside of baking dish and line bottom of dish with buttered wax paper. Fit 1 crêpe, good side down, in the bottom of the dish, and space 4 around the sides (the good sides against dish); cover with a second layer of 4 more overlapping crêpes, as shown.

Spread ¼ of the grated Swiss cheese in the bottom of the dish, cover with the carrots, pressing them well in place, and top with ⅓ of the remaining cheese. Ladle in enough custard mixture to come just to the level of the carrots and cheese. Arrange 1 crêpe on top, and spread over it the mushrooms and another ladleful of custard. Arrange 1 more crêpe over the mushrooms and spread on ½ of the remaining cheese, then the broccoli, and the final bit of cheese. Pour on the last of the custard mixture and fold the first layer of overhanging crêpes up over the filling; cover with a crêpe, fold the outside layer of overhang up over it, and cover with 1 or more crêpes (depending on their size and the top of your dish). Place a round of buttered wax paper over the dish, and cover with a sheet of foil.

1) Lining baking dish, brown side of crêpes against walls

Peel broccoli for color and crispness.

2) Adding custard to first layer of carrots and cheese

I think it best to bake almost immediately, in case the custard leaks against the sides and bottom of the dish, sticking the crêpes to it and making a mess later when you attempt to unmold.

Baking

About 1 ¾ hours

Bake on lower middle rack in preheated oven, placing a pizza pan or something on the rack below to catch possible dribbles. In about 1 hour, when the gâteau has started to rise, turn oven up to 400°F/205°C. It will eventually rise an inch or more (2½ to 3 cm) and is done when a meat thermometer, its point at the center, reads 160°F/71°C. Remove from oven and let rest at room temperature for 10 to 15 minutes, allowing the custard to set and settle. Then run a thin-bladed knife carefully around inside of dish, and unmold onto a hot platter.

Surround the gâteau, if you wish, with fresh tomato sauce. To serve, cut into wedges, as though it were a cake, and spoon sauce around.

May be baked in advance; unmold the gâteau after its wait, and keep it warm in the turned-off oven, covered with an upside-down bowl. In any case, do not let the baked gâteau sit in its baking dish in a hot turned-off oven — as I did (but you did not see!) on our TV show. The cooking liquids leaked into the bottom of the baking dish, evidently, and the hot oven then glued the crêpes to the dish. Fortunately we had a standby gâteau safely loosened from its mold, which replaced my messy unmolding caper on the serving dish. There is indeed nothing like experience as a teacher!

To serve cold

This makes a delicious cold dish for a luncheon or to take on a picnic. Accompany with a tomato or cucumber salad and, if you wish, a sour cream dressing or the same tomato sauce, which also is good cold.

3) Centering crêpe over layer

4) Completing the final layers

Check doneness with an instant meat thermometer.

Ice Cream and a Rum and Meatless Mincemeat Sauce

Serving 6 people

Following the general line of quick and easy but good desserts, here is an idea for using a jar of mincemeat, which is so good it should be eaten more often than just on Thanksgiving. You need no recipe for this, only 1½ quarts (1½ L) or so best-quality vanilla ice cream and half a jar or so of good mincemeat. Place the ice cream in a serving bowl, and heat the mincemeat with several spoonfuls of dark Jamaica rum, or even bourbon whiskey, which is a fine substitute. Spoon the hot mincemeat sauce over each serving (you may wish to heat and flame it at the table), and you may also wish to pass some attractive sugar cookies along with the dessert.

To glamorize the mincemeat, heat it up with rum before serving it on vanilla ice cream.

⏱ Timing

You have little to do at the last minute to serve this meal, and more than half the work is already done if you make it a habit to freeze and stock such staple items as loaves of French bread, stacks of crêpes, grated Swiss cheese, mushroom duxelles, and fresh tomato sauce. Even if you must prepare these things specially for your party, you can do so 2 or 3 days beforehand, freeze the French bread, and store the other items in the refrigerator.

You can steam the spaghetti squash and prepare and cook the carrots and broccoli on the day before your party.

That morning, wash, dry, and refrigerate your salad greens, mix the vinaigrette dressing, compose (and refrigerate) the custard sauce for the gâteau, and cook the eggplant.

Two and a half hours before dinner, assemble the gâteau and start baking it.

Half an hour before serving it, test the gâteau for doneness. At this time you could start warming the mincemeat in a pan of water over low heat. Just before you sit down, unmold the gâteau, and move the ice cream from freezer to refrigerator, to soften, and reheat the eggplant and spaghetti squash and the tomato sauce. Toss your salad just before you serve it.

Menu Variations

All kinds of garnishes are nice with spaghetti squash — or you might use real spaghetti with the eggplant garnish for a main dish, instead of the gâteau. You can vary the gâteau itself by substituting other vegetables in the layers. Or you can make one of the filled crêpe recipes in *Mastering I,* assembling the entire dish in the morning and heating it just before dinner. The fillings can be infinitely varied — try cooked minced chicken sometime, for omnivores, or creamed shellfish — and the crêpes are served beautifully sauced in their baking dish. *J.C. & Co.* has other good toppings for storebought ice cream, and it's easy to think up your own.

J.C.'s Kitchen contains several good recipes for dried legumes, which make hearty main dishes for all vegetarians, including the strictest; if your guests, like ours, will eat eggs and cheese, that opens up a world of soufflés, omelets, and gratins. If, however, your guests are coming not just for a meal but for several days, you may want to look at a specialized vegetarian cookbook. Frances Moore Lappé's *Diet for a Small Planet* (New York: Ballantine Books, rev. ed. 1975) analyzes nonanimal proteins and shows how to boost protein values by combining complementary foods. It contains a lot of recipes, and even more may be found in its companion volume, *Recipes for a Small Planet,* by Ellen Buchman Ewald (New York: Ballantine Books, 1975). Martha Rose Shulman's *The Vegetarian Feast* (New York: Harper & Row, 1978) is concerned with fancier vegetarian cooking and helps out the amateur with a wide choice of menus. Finally, Anna Thomas's two volumes, *The Vegetarian Epicure* (New York: Alfred A. Knopf and Vintage Books, 1972 and 1978, and her recent *The New Vegetarian Epicure,* 1996), have such delicious and well-considered dishes that they belong on the shelf of any blissfully greedy cook of any persuasion including Red Fang.

Leftovers

If you have last-minute no-shows, go ahead and cook all your eggplant, but put some aside before the addition of parsley and garlic. It's the foundation of several splendid dishes (see *Mastering II* and *J.C.'s Kitchen*), some of which you can eat cold. Two versions of eggplant caviar (a puréed spread or dip), one containing walnuts and the other sesame seed paste, are special treats for vegetarians.

With extra cooked vegetables, custard sauce, and cheese, you have the makings of a nice gratin or the filling for a quiche, and of course cooked or uncooked vegetable scraps are a natural for soup. I have no great suggestions for leftover salad. But extra French bread begs to be sliced and toasted for *croûtes* that you can store in the freezer until it's onion soup time again; or blend or process them into crumbs—

a jar of them, kept in the freezer, is a handy resource for any cook.

Leftover mincemeat, of course, makes splendid tarts, pies, and turnovers; since it keeps a long time in the refrigerator, once opened, you need be in no hurry to use it up.

Postscript: R&D in cooking

Certainly, one of the pleasures of cooking is thinking up new ways to present familiar ingredients. You will note that I have borrowed an engineering term rather than using the word "invent" because "invention," to me, means something like producing the very first mayonnaise, or puff pastry, or ice cream. Few cooks achieve such distinction, or have such happy accidents or discoveries. (Who could have known in advance that egg yolks would emulsify, or that flour and fat would separate in the oven into towering, airy layers?) But hardly any of us who cook has not put something together in an unusual, original, or different way, drawing from general knowledge, experience, and imagination.

I think our crêpe and vegetable gâteau could be called a creation, using the term loosely in its meaning of "investing something with a new form." Anyway, the recipe grew out of the combined activities of us cooks on the *J.C. & Co.* team, and we are very pleased with ourselves. I might mention that in our first experiments we baked the gâteau in a bain-marie (pan of water) in a 350°F/180°C oven; it came out beautifully—ideally, rather—but *3 hours* is a very long time, so for the recipe and for television we threw out the water and stepped up the heat. As noted, other cooks might like to fill the layers with other ingredients, keeping our *R* (Research) but continuing with their own *D* (Development). What we're offering you is an attractive idea, not a sacrosanct monument.

A lavish menu for a big crowd —but the single cook can swing it.

Buffet Dinner

An Expandable Menu
For 20 to 30 people or more

Sweet-and-Sour Sausage Nuggets
Tarama Brandade—Carp roe with hints of
garlic, olive oil, and Provençal mysteries
Pissaladière Gargantua—Giant onion and
anchovy pizza
Toasted Pita Triangles; Raw Vegetable
Nibbles; Nuts and Crackers

❧

Braised Pot Roast of Beef—Bottom round of
beef in red wine
Potato Gnocchi—Cheese and potato
dumplings browned in the oven
Old-fashioned Country Ham
A Cauldron of Home-cooked White Beans
with Herbs
Fresh Vegetables à la Grecque—Cold in
aromatic liquid
Tossed Green Salad
Hot French Bread

❧

Orange Bavarian Torte—Dressed in whipped
cream and glazed orange peel
Sliced Strawberries with Orange Liqueur

❧

Suggested wines:
White wine—French colombard or Chablis;
red wine—a Beaujolais, zinfandel, or cabernet.
Champagne or sparkling wine for the dessert

A big bounteous party is fun for the cook the way a herbaceous border is fun for the gardener: you start with a gorgeous vision, make precise plans, execute them leisurely (smugly checking off item by item)—and lo! there it all is, right on time and a sight to behold. You really brought it off. Even for 30 people, this grand spread is entirely feasible for 1 cook. On this menu, the braised beef and the torte each serve 15, and the other recipes are for 10; so, for say 30 guests, braise 2 rounds, make 2 cakes, and otherwise multiply by 3.

Here's how I set party priorities:
1) *The End Result. Flavor*—will the meal be delicious, with each dish at its best? (This eliminates many pastas and hot fish things, which should be eaten soon after their preparation. At a very large buffet, plan on dishes that can sit around a bit.) *Appearance*—will everything look handsome and stay that way? By this token, do your own carving and slicing at table, or else appoint a friend to take it on; otherwise you'll have Devastated Areas. *Space*—if you haven't much, serve compact dishes, pots not platters. If you have lots, use several locations: one for appetizers, one for the main course, one for dessert. This keeps people moving and mingling, for one thing. *Temperature*—have you enough warming devices, and enough electric outlets to serve them? You can't use 2 on the same line, unless one is a low-voltage slow cooker. However, thick-walled casseroles stay warm a long time, and there are always chafing dishes and candle-heated stands. Have plenty of ice around for cooling wines and filling insulated chests, etc.

2) *Space* – not just for serving, but for storing dishes prepared in advance, and, before that, their components. Most refrigerators need a periodic clear out, and now's a good time. Anyway, we could all use our refrigerators more efficiently. Cake layers can be stacked with racks or strong cardboard in between. Square containers are more efficient than round ones. Flexible containers, such as plastic bags, fit anywhere. (A tip: having dried your salad makings, tear the greens and assemble the whole salad in 1 bag.) In winter, the back porch makes a good refrigerator annex; in summer, an insulated chest; perhaps your friends have space you can borrow.

3) *Equipment*—friends and space both count here. To my mind, it's pointless to have more than one rarely used, expensive, or space-consuming item per neighborhood. So why not a community duck press, lobster pot, fish steamer, *pâté en croûte* mold, spring-form pan? A portable tabletop oven is another very useful community item, as are slow cookers and electric hot trays. For the ham on this menu, as for, say, *gravlaks,* you need a fine slicing knife—expensive and not used every day—so share it! If you have only 1 oven, plan on dishes that can co-occupy it (cakes and soufflés can't), and that require the same temperature setting.

On ordinary staple equipment, my advice is not to stint yourself. Have plenty of bowls, strainers, spatulas, paring knives, and kitchen towels, so you don't have to waste time on petty calculations, or stop to wash single items.

4) *Rhythm and Timing.* It's very helpful to start a cooking bout by "doing your prep," as restaurant cooks say: squeezing lemon juice (keep refrigerated), chopping parsley, washing and drying salad greens, putting a kettle on to boil, starting a new batch of ice cubes. White wine can be chilled all day; red wine can be brought to room temperature early. Time savers: large flour, sugar, and salt containers, each with its own rarely washed set of measuring cups or spoons—otherwise, every time you open a package, you have to mop up spilled

grains; a big pan of soapy water where used implements can soak; a portable pastry slab you can chill. Always read a recipe through beforehand, and assemble all the items and equipment before starting. Measure the capacity of molds and baking pans, and mark them.

Make and freeze "standard parts" like doughs, crêpes, and stock beforehand, and plan jobs for the time when something can simmer or bake unattended. (I know lots of cooks who budget their time but not their energy.) A job that takes 10 minutes when you're fresh can take 20 when you're not; you'll wind up livelier if you alternate sitting jobs with standing ones, chopping with paring, etc. Clutter is fatiguing; for me, frequent cleanups are more restful than one final bout.

5) *Cost Effectiveness*—really, Effort Effectiveness. Now, with a big party, is not the time to put in 100 percent more work for 5 percent more effect. Take this simple but sound braised beef. Old-fashioned recipes call for larding, marination, and a sauce slowly reduced to almost nothing, then reconstituted with wine. This is all very well if you've nothing else to do; but basically what gives a braise flavor and tenderness is cooking and keeping meat and liquid together. Reheating this dish is not merely a convenience but an improvement.

On the other hand, put your effort where it does count. Whipped cream, for instance, is much better made by hand, over ice, than with a mixer; a custard sauce can't be beaten mechanically—so much foam builds up that you can't see what you're doing. You could use machines, in this menu, for making pastry, cutting onions, mixing the *brandade* and the gnocchi, and whipping egg whites, but it's not really a menu planned for machines.

6) *Resources*, and Your Own Resourcefulness. There's usually more than one way to skin a rabbit; the Timing section of this chapter gives you only one. However you go at it, you can do this meal alone, and so well in advance that, at the time of your party, your kitchen can be sparkling, uncluttered, and all ready for a glorious evening.

Preparations and Marketing

Recommended Equipment:

Serving: let's suppose you're planning for 20 or 30 people, and for the full menu. You have first to decide whether to carve the beef and the ham at table, and if you do, that means 1 or 2 large carving boards, and, for the ham, a first-rate, razor-sharp slicing knife. The ham is served cold or cool; the beef is best hot but is still good at room temperature. The sausage nuggets and the beans will stay warm in slow cookers, or you can use warming devices; 1 big electric tray would hold them, plus the gnocchi. Freshly baked *pissaladière* will probably be eaten before it cools off! Allow space for your big salad bowl, your platter of cold vegetables, and your smaller bowls of *brandade*, raw vegetables, nuts, crackers, and pita triangles—plus more space for dessert, sauce, dessert plates, your bar setup, and your coffee tray. Remember that carvers need elbow room, and consider the number and location of electric outlets for warmers. At one efficient buffet served in a roomy kitchen, I remember hot dishes were served from the counter tops, and cold ones were bedded on ice in the sink; used dishes and silver were slid—gently and unobtrusively—into trash barrels filled with soapy water, to soak. A cooled-off oven also makes a discreet repository for such items, as does your dishwashing or laundry machine.

Be sure your knife is really sharp before you start slicing the beef.

Cooking: if you did each job in succession, using a minimum of pans, you'd need 1 skillet (preferably nonstick) for sausages and the pizza onions, and 1 large, heavy, stainless-steel saucepan to sauce sausages, simmer black olives, poach gnocchi, cook vegetables, and make custard sauce (the reason why it has to be stainless). For baking gnocchi and *pissaladière*, you need 2 jelly-roll pans (1 of which browned the beef), or 1, plus a baking sheet. A large, deep roaster, preferably with cover, will cook first the ham, then the beef. A food processor or mixer will help with several jobs. You need a casserole for the beans and a deep pan for the torte (10- by 3-inch, or 25- by 8-cm, spring-form preferred).

Be sure to check your supply of aluminum foil, plastic wrap, plastic bags, white kitchen string, and cheesecloth. Small implements needed: meat thermometer, pastry bag with large star tube, skimmer or slotted spoon, giant spatula and flexible-blade spatula.

Obviously, the more saucepans, bowls, sieves, colanders, and paring knives you have, the faster you can go.

Staples to Have on Hand:

Salt
White and black peppercorns
Granulated sugar
Eggs (17 "large")
Butter (1½ pounds or 675 g)
Confectioners sugar (½ cup or 70 g)
Dried herbs: oregano, thyme, allspice berries, imported bay leaves, whole cloves, mustard seeds, coriander, saffron threads, and fennel seeds; mixed herbs (optional)
Grated nutmeg
Pure vanilla extract
Olive oil
Cooking oil, or rendered beef or pork fat
Wine vinegar
Soy sauce
Hot pepper sauce
Dijon-type prepared mustard
Cream of tartar
Arrowroot, or rice flour, or potato flour, or cornstarch

All-purpose flour
Milk (2¼ cups or 5½ dL)
Butter, clarified (about ½ cup or 1 dL)
Grated Gruyère, Parmesan, or Swiss cheese
        (1¼ cups; 5 ounces or 140 g)
Beef stock or bouillon (5 cups or 1¼ L)
White nonsweet bread for crumbs (½ loaf)
Lemons (3)
Carrots (1 bunch)
Celery (1 bunch)
Garlic (1 head)
Parsley (1 large bunch)
Red wine (1 bottle; see beef recipe)
Orange liqueur (3 Tb; plus 7 to 8 Tb, optional)
Optional: concentrated frozen orange juice

Specific Ingredients for This Menu:

Excellent sausage meat (1 pound or 450 g) ▼
Bottom round of beef (1 whole trimmed, 10 to
        12 pounds or 4½ to 5½ kg)
Country ham (1 whole; see recipe)
Chilled pastry dough (1½ pounds or 675 g) ▼
Gelatin (6 Tb or 6 envelopes)
Flat anchovy fillets, packed in olive oil (two 2-
        ounce or 60-g cans) ▼
Black Mediterranean-type or Niçoise olives
        (about 24) ▼
Dry white beans (1 pound or 450 g)
Optional: fresh basil (1 bunch)
Apricot jam or chutney (4 Tb)
Tarama (salt carp roe) (½ cup or 115 g) ▼
Heavy cream (5 half pints, or 1¼ L plus)

Orange juice (1 ⅓ cups or 3 ¼ dL)
Oranges (3)
Optional: candied orange peel
Cakes: *génoise*, yellow, or sponge (can be
    storebought; 2 round, about 10 by 1
    inches or 25 by 2.5 cm, see page 105)
Vegetables for cold platter (see recipe)
Vegetables for raw nibbles
Greens for salad
Potatoes (about 6½ pounds or 3 kg; or can be
    instant—see recipe)
Yellow onions (about 3 pounds or 1350 g)
Ingredients for dessert sauce (see recipe)
Nuts, crackers, pita bread, etc. (ad lib)
Plenty of ice cubes for cooling wine, etc.

Remarks:

Sausage meat: a quick easy recipe for making your own is on page 110. *Pie crust dough:* double the proportions for the pie and quiche dough on page 110. *Anchovy fillets:* don't use if decorating *pissaladière* in advance; use more olives. Always open anchovy cans at the last minute. *Olives:* the salt-and-oil-cured Mediterranean type need blanching before you use them, to remove excess salt—simmer in 1 quart (1 L) water 5 to 10 minutes (depending on how salty they are), drain, and rinse. If you don't like to serve olives with pits, you'll either have to pit them or switch to the relatively tasteless pitted black olives you can buy in any market. *Tarama:* this is a salty orange-pink paste, often imported from Greece, that is sold in Middle Eastern markets and delicatessens.

Onion pizza will be decorated with olives and anchovies.

Sweet-and-Sour Sausage Nuggets

You will note the perhaps odd addition of aspic to the sausage mixture here, a suggestion from chef Joe E. Hyde. His disciple, our own chef Marian, says *he* says the aspic makes the meatballs lighter, and indeed it does, since these have a delightfully unheavy texture.

For about 24 nuggets

The Sausage Mixture:

1 pound (450 g) best-quality well-seasoned prepared sausage meat

1 "large" egg

5 Tb crumbs from fresh white nonsweet bread with body

4 Tb strong liquefied aspic (a scant teaspoon plain unflavored gelatin, softened and then heated to dissolve in 4 Tb consommé)

The Sweet-and-Sour Sauce:

¾ cup (1 ¾ dL) well-flavored beef stock or broth

1 Tb wine vinegar

4 Tb strained apricot jam or chutney

1 Tb arrowroot, rice flour, potato flour, or cornstarch dissolved in 5 Tb orange juice

1 Tb soy sauce

1 Tb butter

1 Tb Dijon-type prepared mustard

6 drops hot pepper sauce

Salt and freshly ground black pepper

Beat the sausage meat, egg, crumbs, and aspic together in a bowl. If too soft to form, chill for half an hour or so, or beat over ice. Using 1½ tablespoons of meat at a time, form into balls. Chill for 30 minutes. Brown slowly in a large, preferably nonstick skillet, and drain on paper towels.

Meanwhile, blend the sauce ingredients together in a large, heavy stainless-steel saucepan; simmer 3 to 4 minutes, and correct seasoning, adding salt and pepper to taste, and drops more of the listed ingredients if you think them necessary. Fold the sausage into the sauce.

🕐 May be done a day or so in advance.

To serve

Reheat to the simmer for a minute or 2, then place in a decorative bowl or pan and set on an electric warmer, or in a pan of water over a chafing dish flame. Have a container of toothpicks at hand, for spearing.

Sweet-and-sour sausage nuggets stay warm over a water bath set on a chafing dish burner.

Tarama Brandade

A spread or dip—salted carp roe puréed with potato, garlic, olive oil, cream, and seasonings

The most famous *brandade* (it literally means "stirred vigorously") is a purée of salt cod, garlic, and olive oil, a marvelous concoction that originated in Provence, and there is every reason to put that brilliant concept to good use with other ingredients. The pink and salty carp roe, the kind you find in jars in Middle Eastern groceries, is a fine example. It is usually whipped up with soaked bread crumbs, but mashed potato makes an even smoother and more delicious mixture.

For about 1 quart (1 L)

2½ cups (6 dL) warm cooked potatoes (baked, preferably, or boiled, or stiff instant mashed)

½ cup (115 g) tarama (salt carp roe)

1 or more cloves garlic, puréed

½ cup (1 dL) fruity olive oil

½ cup (1 dL) heavy cream

Fresh lemon juice to taste

Freshly ground white pepper

Drops of hot pepper sauce

Equipment:

A food processor makes quick work here; or use an electric mixer; or a potato ricer or vegetable mill, mixing bowl, and wooden spoon.

If you are using a processor, purée the potatoes, using the steel blade, then add the *tarama* and puréed garlic and continue processing while you add olive oil alternating with cream to make a heavy creamy paste that holds its shape lightly when lifted in a spoon. Season to taste with lemon juice, pepper, and hot pepper sauce plus a little more oil, cream, and/or garlic if you think them needed. (Otherwise, purée the potatoes and whip in the *tarama* and garlic, then the oil alternating with the cream, and finally the seasonings.) Pack into a serving bowl, or chill and mound on a serving dish as shown here.

🕐 May be made several days in advance; cover and refrigerate.

Variations:

Brandade de morue—purée with salt cod
Substitute 1 pound (450 g) cooked salt cod for the *tarama,* warming it first in a saucepan over moderate heat with 4 tablespoons olive oil, and beating with a large fork to shred it. Then purée with 1½ cups (3½ dL) cooked potato and 2 or more cloves garlic, puréed, adding alternate dollops of olive oil and cream, and seasoning with salt, pepper, and lemon juice. A marvelous mixture.

Avocado brandade
Use equal amounts of warm cooked potato and ripe avocado, puréeing them together with a small clove of garlic, puréed, and adding spoonfuls of heavy cream and olive oil. Season with salt, white pepper, and lemon juice. Makes a beautiful pale-green creamy dip that keeps nicely in a covered jar in the refrigerator for a day or 2. I have added anchovies, chives, and capers to it, but I think the simpler version is more successful.

A rubber spatula makes decorative swirls on a mounded surface of tarama brandade.

Pissaladière Gargantua

A party-sized onion and anchovy pizza

I always like to have a pastry something for large gatherings, and the pizza idea in rectangular form is a good one because it is not too rich—no eggs, just pie crust dough, cooked onions, anchovies, black olives, and a sprinkling of cheese for the top. Another plus is that you can assemble and freeze it, all except for the anchovy topping. Furthermore, 1 large sheet of it will give you 20 generous portions, or 40 small ones.

For 20 appetizer-sized servings

4 cups (1 L) sliced yellow onions
4 to 6 Tb olive oil
Chilled pie crust dough (proportions for 3½ cups, 1 pound, or 454 g flour; double the recipe on page 110)
Salt and pepper
1 tsp or so dried oregano or thyme, or mixed dried herbs
Two 2-ounce (60-g) cans flat anchovy fillets, packed in olive oil
About 24 black olives (the dried Mediterranean type or other salty imported smallish black olives)
About ½ cup (1 dL) grated Parmesan cheese, or mixed cheeses

Equipment:

A jelly-roll pan, nonstick preferred, about 11 by 17 inches (28 by 43 cm)

Cook the onions slowly in 4 tablespoons of olive oil in a roomy covered frying pan or saucepan, stirring frequently, until they are soft and thoroughly tender, but not browned —20 minutes or more.

🕐 May be cooked ahead; cool, cover, and refrigerate for several days, or freeze.

Meanwhile, butter the bottom (not the sides) of the jelly-roll pan. Rapidly roll out the chilled dough into a rectangle ⅛ inch (½ cm) thick, and larger and wider than the pan. Fit it into the pan, and neatly trim off the overhanging edges. Fold edges of dough down against bottom all around; press a decorative border into them with the tines of a table fork. Prick inside surface of dough all over with 2 forks, as shown—to keep it from rising up during baking.

🕐   Cover and refrigerate (or freeze) until you are ready to continue.

When onions are tender, season carefully with salt and pepper, and either let them cool or stir over cold water until cool. Spread them over the inside surface of the dough.

🕐   Cover and refrigerate (or freeze) until you are ready to continue.

Baking

25 to 30 minutes at 425°F/220°C

While the oven is preheating, arrange a design of anchovies, such as the diagonal pattern illustrated, over the onions, with black olives at strategic intervals. Sprinkle the cheese over the onions and the design, and dribble on a tablespoon of olive oil (oil from the anchovy can, if you wish). Bake in lower third level of oven (where pastry will crisp better) until pastry has browned and is beginning to shrink from the sides of the pan.

Serving

Slide onto a serving board or work surface, and either let guests cut their own, or cut into serving pieces and arrange on a plate. Five strips across the *pissaladière* and 4 the length of it give you 20 pieces.

Assembling the anchovy and onion pizza

🕐 I prefer not to arrange the anchovies more than 30 minutes or so before baking because I think they develop an off taste if they sit around out of their hermetically sealed can. And although it can be baked ahead, the *pissaladière* is at its most delicious served fresh and warm, rather than cold.

Variations:

Pizza

Use a regular pizza topping of tomato sauce, herbs, and cheese, plus, if you wish, diced cooked mushrooms, sausages, ham, and so forth. An interesting pizza additive is diced sautéed eggplant (use the recipe on page 78, the garnish for our spaghetti squash).

Quiche

If you want a cheese and cream combination, which can be very good too, you will have either to make a prebaked crust with edging to hold the liquid quiche mixture or do as follows. Spread the surface of the dough with shaved or coarsely grated Swiss cheese, using about 2 cups (½ L). Beat 1 egg and 2 yolks in a bowl with ⅔ cup (1½ dL) heavy cream, season well with pepper, drops of Worcestershire, and a little sage or thyme. Just before baking, spread the egg and cream mixture over the cheese—it is to be a thick coating only; if you need more liquid, spread on a little more cream. Bake as described for the *pissaladière.* This makes attractively brown and cheesy mouthfuls.

Cocktail Miscellany

You will want the usual crackers and nuts, and something like potato chips or toasted pita triangles, plus some raw vegetable nibbles for those who are well-disciplined dieters. Since every household has its favorites, I shall not go into details.

Notes on the Braising of Beef

Beef cuts for braising

I like the bottom round for braising—the long outside muscle of the leg; it is a solid piece with no separations, and it cuts into neat pieces. Other braising parts, like chuck, top round, and tip (or face), break into separate muscles, and that makes for messy carving. The brisket is a possibility, but not my favorite for this dish, and I have never cared for the stringy quality of the usually overpriced eye of the round.

If you are braising more than one

You will need either 2 covered roasting pans unless you have a mammoth one that will hold 2 beef bottoms, or you can braise the roasts 1 at a time, and cool 1 while you are cooking the other—or others. You can braise the meat on top of the stove if you are careful with the heat, and turn the meat every 45 minutes or so, but an oven is more even—2 ovens are ideal.

The red wine sauce for the beef

Any meat that needs long simmering, as in a braise or a stew, wants some kind of a sauce. The meat is no longer moist after cooking because its juices have gone into the braising liquid: both meat and liquid take from and give to each other, which is one of the principal reasons that braised meat has such fine flavor. In this recipe the braising liquid is lightly thickened; when the beef is done the sauce is made.

Bottom round of beef

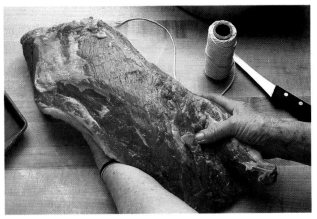

Braised Pot Roast of Beef

Daube de boeuf—Boeuf à la mode
Whole bottom round of beef braised in
red wine

A fine large pot roast of beef is ideal for a group because you can cook it 1 or 2 days before serving. In fact, it is better that you do so because the meat not only will pick up additional flavor from sitting in its braising juices but will also slice more neatly, since the meat fibers will have compacted themselves as they cool, and will hold together nicely when reheated. Furthermore, braised beef is easy to cook, and it stands up well during the leisurely pace of most buffets.

For a 10- to 12-pound (4 ½- to 5 ½-kg)
roast, serving 15 to 20 people

A whole trimmed bottom round of beef (10 to 12 pounds or 4½ to 5½ kg)

Rendered beef or pork fat, or cooking oil

6 Tb all-purpose flour

About 4 cups (1 L) beef stock or best-quality canned beef bouillon

Salt

2 carrots, roughly chopped

2 large onions, roughly chopped

1 large celery stalk, roughly chopped

4 cloves garlic, not peeled

1 large herb bouquet (10 parsley sprigs, 3 or 4 imported bay leaves, 1 tsp thyme, 6 allspice berries, all tied in washed cheesecloth)

1 bottle healthy young red wine, like zinfandel, Chianti, or other of like quality

Equipment:

White string for tying the beef; a jelly-roll pan for browning it; a medium-sized heavy-bottomed saucepan, for starting the sauce base; a covered roaster, or a large roasting pan with sides 3 to 4 inches (8 to 10 cm) high and heavy aluminum foil

Browning the beef
Wind white string around the beef down its length, to hold the meat in place firmly during its cooking. Paint on all sides with fat or oil, set in the jelly-roll pan, and brown slowly on all sides under the broiler, being careful not to let the meat burn. This is a process that needs close watching, but it is the easiest way to brown such a large piece.

🕐   May be browned well in advance, if need be, and especially if you are doing more than 1 roast.

Preliminaries for the sauce base
Meanwhile, but keeping your eye on the beef as well, blend 5 tablespoons fat or oil in the heavy saucepan with the flour (if you are doing more than 1 bottom, double or triple this amount), and stir almost continuously, but rather slowly, with a wooden spoon over moderate heat as the flour gradually turns a quite dark nutty brown. Making a brown *roux* takes time and care—you don't want the flour to burn, just to darken slowly so it will not have a bitter taste. Time: about 10 minutes. Remove from heat and let cool several minutes, then blend in the beef stock and set aside.

Braising the beef
2 ½ to 3 hours
Preheat oven to 350°F/180°C. Salt the meat on all sides, using about 2 teaspoons, and set it in the roaster fat side up. Arrange the vegetables and garlic around the meat, add the herb bouquet, and pour in the wine and the beef stock—*roux*, plus a little more stock if neces-

Use a good healthy young red wine for your beef.

sary, to come almost halfway up the meat. Bring to the simmer on top of the stove; cover and set in lower third of oven. When contents are bubbling quietly, in about half an hour, baste the meat with the sauce and turn thermostat down to 325°F/165°C. Liquid should simmer quietly throughout the cooking; regulate oven accordingly. Baste and check on the cooking every half hour until 2 hours are up, then begin testing. The meat is done when a sharp-pronged fork can penetrate through the middle section with comparative ease. If you have any doubts, cut a piece off the large end and eat it: the meat should be somewhat firm, but not tough. Time of cooking will depend on quality of meat—a Prime well-aged piece will take a shorter cooking time, while a fresh Choice cut may take up to an hour longer.

⏱ Meat may be carved and served after a rest of half an hour or so, but is really better cooked several hours or a day in advance.

Finishing Meat and Sauce:
Let the beef cool for half an hour, basting it every 10 minutes or so with the sauce, and turning it several times. Then remove it and drain contents of roaster through a colander or sieve into a large saucepan, pressing juices out of braising vegetables into pan. Bring liquid to the simmer, skimming fat off surface as you do so; continue to skim for several minutes as fat rises to the surface while sauce very slowly bubbles. You can serve it now, but the sauce will really taste best if you have time to keep simmering and skimming it for half an hour as it slowly reduces. Taste carefully for seasoning and strength, and boil down slowly until the sauce coats a spoon just enough so you know it will coat the meat. (If by any chance sauce is strong and fine but not thick enough, soften 2 or more tablespoons of arrowroot, rice flour, potato flour, or cornstarch—or even all-purpose flour—in several spoons of wine or stock; remove sauce from heat, beat in starch mixture, then simmer for 2 to 3 minutes. On the other hand, if sauce is too thick, thin out with more stock.)

Pour the sauce around the meat, cover with foil or wax paper, and refrigerate.

Reheating and Serving:
You may reheat the beef whole, as is, or sliced and sauced. Here are the two alternatives.

To reheat the beef whole
Cover the beef closely and reheat either in the oven at around 300°F/150°C, or by simmering very slowly over low heat on top of the stove, turning the beef every 15 minutes. It will take 30 to 40 minutes to reheat, and the internal temperature need be no more than 120°F/49°C. It is important that you do not let the meat overheat and overcook, as it will fall apart when sliced. However, you may keep it warm once it is reheated. Just before serving, cut and discard the trussing strings.

Carving at the table. If you have reheated the beef whole and there is a willing carver available, it is always appealing to have meat sliced at the table. Set the beef on a handsome board, and have the carver start his work at the large end, as illustrated, making bias slices, since a straight cut across the meat would make too large a piece for 1 serving. When he gets near the tail end and notices any overt tendency to shredding, he cuts the meat into chunks. He should have a bowl of sauce on a hotplate at his side, and will ladle a spoonful or so over each serving.

Carved meat presented on a platter
Carve the meat in the kitchen and return it neatly to the roaster or a large baking pan; baste with the sauce. Let it warm through slowly, and keep it warm, then arrange it on a hot platter with sauce over each piece, renewing with meat and sauce as necessary.

Bottom round can be cut into neat bias slices.

Potato Gnocchi

Cheese and potato dumplings

Although the gnocchi is of Italian origin, when it came to France it turned into a dumpling, at least in this version, where it consists of mashed potatoes, cheese, and a *pâte à choux* (a heavy eggy white sauce that swells when baked). You give them a preliminary poaching in salted water, after which the gnocchi may be refrigerated or frozen; to serve, you brown them in the oven. For a starchy something to go with a party meal such as this, I think the gnocchi are a fine solution just because of their amenability. Besides, they make good eating with the braised beef and its red wine sauce.

For about 30 golfball-sized gnocchi

For the Pâte à Choux:
About 2 cups (½ L)

1 cup (¼ L) water

6 Tb (3 ounces or 85 g) butter

1 tsp salt

¾ cup (3½ ounces or 100 g) all-purpose flour (measure by dipping dry-measure cups into flour and sweeping off excess)

3 "large" eggs, plus ½ to 1 more egg if needed

Other Ingredients:

4 cups (1 L) firm warm mashed potatoes (see notes in recipe)

¾ cup (3 ounces or 85 g) finely grated Gruyère, Parmesan, or mixed cheese

A pinch of nutmeg

Salt and pepper

A little flour, for forming gnocchi

½ cup (1 dL) clarified butter, more if needed

Equipment:

A heavy 2-quart (2-L) saucepan; a wooden spatula or spoon; a hand-held electric mixer or a food processor is useful; 1 or 2 wide casseroles or saucepans, for poaching the gnocchi; a large bowl of cold water; a skimmer or slotted spoon; nonstick baking pans

The Pâte à Choux:
Measure out the ingredients listed. Bring the water to the boil in the 2-quart (2-L) saucepan, meanwhile cutting the butter in pieces and dropping it in, along with the salt. When water is boiling and butter has melted, remove pan from heat and immediately pour in all the flour at once, beating vigorously with wooden spatula to blend. Set over moderate heat, beating, until pastry cleans itself off sides and bottom of pan and begins to film the bottom of the pan. Beat for 2 minutes or so over moderately low heat to evaporate excess moisture. Remove from heat.

If you are continuing by hand or with a mixer, make a well in the center of the hot pastry with your spatula or mixer, break an egg into the well, and vigorously beat it in until absorbed. Continue with the next 2 eggs, one by one. Mixture should be quite stiff, but if too firm for easy beating, break remaining egg into a bowl, beat to blend, and beat driblets into the pastry to loosen it.

If you are using a processor, scrape the hot pastry into the container fitted with the steel blade. Turn on the machine and break the 3 eggs into it, one after the other. Stop the machine, test pastry for consistency, and add the fourth egg by driblets if pastry seems too stiff.

Gnocchi—browned, cheesy dumplings—garnish our platter of braised beef.

⏱ Pastry should be warm when you use it; set over warm but not hot water, and cover loosely. (If pastry is kept too warm the eggs will cook, and lose their puffing abilities.)

The potatoes

Either use plain mashed potatoes here, boiling, peeling, and putting them through a ricer, or use instant mashed, which work perfectly well in this instance; when making them, use the amount of milk specified on the package, a little less of the water, and no butter. Potatoes should be quite stiff.

Combining, forming, and poaching the gnocchi

Bring 3 inches (8 cm) salted water to the simmer in the poaching pans. Beat the warm pastry and warm mashed potatoes together to blend; beat in the cheese, nutmeg, and salt and pepper to taste. Flour your hands, and with a light touch, rapidly roll gobs of the gnocchi mixture into balls 1¾ to 2 inches (4½ to 5 cm) in diameter, and drop into the water. (A sticky business!) Maintain water almost but not quite at the simmer (not bubbling) throughout the cooking—an actual simmer or boil can disintegrate the gnocchi. Gnocchi are done in about 15 minutes, when they have risen to the surface and roll over very easily. Transfer them with the skimmer to the bowl of cold water, and in a minute or so they will sink to the bottom—the cold water firms them and sets the cooking. Remove and drain on a towel.

⏱ The gnocchi may be prepared in advance to this point. Let them dry for half an hour, then chill for an hour. When thoroughly cold, arrange in a roasting pan between layers of plastic wrap; they will keep in the refrigerator 2 to 3 days, or may be frozen.

To serve gnocchi

20 to 30 minutes at 350°F/180°C
(The gnocchi need a final baking in the oven, and the conventional system is to arrange them in a buttered baking-and-serving dish with a covering of grated cheese and butter, or cheese sauce. Here, however, since they are to take the place of potatoes, they are rolled in butter and baked on nonstick aluminum jelly-roll pans or pastry sheets so that they can be lifted off and placed on the meat platter for easy serving.)

Preheat oven, and heat the clarified butter to liquefy it; pour the butter into a dish or pie plate. Roll the gnocchi, a few at a time, in the butter, draining off excess with a slotted spoon. Arrange them ½ inch (1½ cm) apart on the pans and brown lightly in upper and middle third levels of the preheated oven, switching pans from one level to another for even cooking. The gnocchi are done when they have swelled gently, and they usually crack open a little bit; if they do not brown lightly on top, set for a few minutes under a moderate broiler, watching carefully that they do not brown too much.

⏱ May be kept warm for 20 minutes or more, but do not cover them . . . warm potatoes need air circulation.

Transfer poached gnocchi (bottom) to a bowl of cold water to firm them.

Old-fashioned Country Ham

Old Virginia Hams and Smithfield Hams:

These are very special hams, slow cured in the old-fashioned way and with a much drier, saltier, and more intense flavor than ordinary storebought hams. They are usually served cold, sliced paper thin, and make a delicious accompaniment to other dishes on a buffet table. I am particularly partial to a fine old ham served along with the remains of the Thanksgiving turkey, but here, on our buffet, the ham can take the place of a second helping of beef, to eat with the beans, or with bread and cheese.

Country Hams versus Virginia and Smithfield Hams:

What is the difference? Smithfield is easy: by law it can only be called a Smithfield ham if it has been processed in Smithfield, Virginia, by the Smithfield method—a dry salt cure followed by a coating of pepper, a long slow hickory smoking, and a final aging of up to a year or more. And the Smithfield hams have a different look from other hams because Smithfield hogs are of a special breed that produces longer and thinner hams. In addition, if the hogs are fed in the approved manner, they have a unique flavor because of the acorns and hickory nuts, among other delicacies, that make up their diet. A number of Virginia processors outside Smithfield produce the same kind of hams using the same type of hogs, feed, and methods; however, they must content themselves with the name "old Virginia" or "Smithfield type."

"The name Country Ham covers a multitude of sins," writes Colonel Bill Newsom of Kentucky, and he goes on to say that the Kentuckian's definition of a real country ham is one that is dry cured using salt and sugar, then smoked with hickory wood, and aged for 6 months or more. Todd's of Richmond, however, do not age their country hams, since in their opinion an aged ham does not lend itself to slicing thick and frying. In other words, you have to know your country hams because they differ widely in their manner of cure and in their aging. In general, though, I think it is true to say that the Virginias and Smithfields are older, drier, and saltier, as well as thinner and longer, than the country hams, and are really in a category by themselves.

Cooking Procedures:

An aged ham is not difficult to cook—a bit long and cumbersome perhaps, but not a tricky business. First you scrub it with a stiff brush under warm running water to remove any of the harmless mold that has collected on it due to its aging, and with it any pepper and other curing elements embedded in the surface. Then you soak it for a number of hours, depending on its type, to remove some of its salt. It is now ready to cook, either by simmering, or baking, or by a combination of both. When cooked, you slice off the rind and excess fat and, if you wish, you can bone it. Finally, to dress it up, you glaze it in a very hot oven either just as it is, or coated with bread crumbs, or brown sugar, or cloves, etc. A cooked dry-cured aged ham will keep nicely in the refrigerator for several weeks at least.

The exact details of its cooking are, of course, a matter of pride, family tradition, and very definite opinions among Southern cooks, and I have no intention of pontificating on the subject. I have, nonetheless, cooked a good 2 dozen of these hams through the years and have some observations to offer. In the first place, anyone tackling this type of ham will do well to follow the directions of the packer, at least the first time, but keep notes on your results because next time you may want to change things a little, as I have.

Soaking

Soaking softens an aged ham to some extent, and does indeed remove a certain amount of saltiness. Packers' directions vary from 4 to 6 hours for many country hams on up to 48 hours for Smithfield types. I frankly do not like too salty a ham; I soak Smithfields for 3 to 4 days, and aged country hams for 2.

Simmering versus baking

Simmering (or "boiling") a ham takes a large container and a lot of water, but it does remove excess saltiness to quite an extent, and does make a slightly softer ham of a well-aged one. The usual rule is to simmer the ham about 20 minutes per pound (450 g), or until the bones from the hock (small end) can be pulled out of the ham.

The on-again-off-again baking system. Not too long ago an alternate method to simmering was developed. You put your scrubbed and soaked ham, fat side up, in a covered roasting pan with 5 cups (1¼ L) water, or part water and part wine or cider vinegar. You seal the roaster as airtight as you can with a sheet of aluminum foil, cover it, and set it in the oven, bringing the temperature up to 500°F/ 260°C (some say to 400 or 450°F/205 or 230°C). When it has reached that temperature, you time it for exactly 20 minutes, then turn the oven off. Do not open the oven door! Leave for 3 hours. Repeat the heating again, for 20 minutes. Turn the oven off. Do not open the oven door! Leave for 6 to 8 hours or overnight.

I have done several Smithfield-type hams this way; it works, and it is certainly easier than simmering a ham in all that water. But I shall not do it again for a country ham because the heat was too intense or prolonged or inappropriate for one I did recently that had not been aged—it shredded a bit around the edges. My last aged country ham, a buxom chunky beauty from Kentucky, was, I thought, a little too salty and too firm after this cooking.

Combination simmer-bake. For my next aged country ham I shall try simmering it for 10 minutes per pound (450 g), or half the usual time, then baking it in a tightly closed roaster with half a bottle or so each Madeira wine and dry white French vermouth. I'll bake it slowly at 300–325°F/150–165°C for about 1½ hours or to a meat thermometer reading of 160°F/71°C. Sounds like just the right system, and I hope it is.

Tough Edges and Bottoms:

I have asked several ham authorities why some aged hams have such hard bottom and side surfaces (those not covered by fat or rind). The hardening of the "face," as these parts are called in the trade, is a characteristic of the hams, and comes from salting, drying, and just plain old age. You may wish to trim off these hard surfaces before soaking the ham, or after cooking it. A crusty surface makes carving difficult, certainly, and although it seems as though you are removing a lot of meat as you trim it off, you are saving yourself a good deal of trouble when you come to slice and serve. Save the trimmings for flavoring bean or split pea soups, and those that are not too crusty can be ground up with a little of the ham fat to make a tasty ham spread for sandwiches.

To Carve the Ham:

It is a help in carving to pull out the hip bone from underneath the ham before that meat has cooled. Some carvers prefer the cross-grain cut, going straight down at right angles from the surface of the ham to the bone, after having cut an opening wedge out of the hock (small) end. Or slice parallel to the bone and the surface of the meat; start with a wedge taken out of the hock, then slice on the right, then on the left side of the main leg bone.

Aged ham should be cut into the thinnest possible slices. You need a long, sharp knife, and don't saw at the meat; try for long, even strokes the length of the blade.

Mail-Order Hams: See page 109.

White Beans with Herbs

For almost 2 quarts (2 L), serving 10 to 15 people

1 pound (450 g) dry white beans
2 quarts (2 L) water
1 large onion stuck with 2 cloves
1 herb bouquet (6 parsley sprigs, 2 cloves garlic, ¼ tsp thyme, and 1 imported bay leaf tied together in washed cheesecloth)
2 tsp salt
1 stick (4 ounces or 115 g) butter (optional)
3 or 4 cloves garlic puréed with 1 tsp salt
5 to 6 Tb minced fresh parsley and/or basil
Bean cooking juices as needed
Salt and pepper

Cook the beans with the water, onion, herb bouquet, and salt, as described on page 64 (halving the recipe and omitting the pork). Shortly before serving, rewarm them if necessary. Melt the butter in a large serving casserole, stir in the garlic and let warm a moment, then fold in the beans and fresh herbs plus a little of the bean cooking juices if you feel them needed. Season carefully to taste. (If you omit the butter, simmer the garlic for a few minutes in a little of the bean cooking juices.)

🕐   May be kept warm on an electric hotplate.

Doubling and Tripling the Recipe:
Since a large quantity is often difficult to handle and to season properly, you are probably better off finishing and flavoring the beans in batches about this size, then combining them.

Fresh Vegetables à la Grecque

A selection of vegetables cooked in an herbal marinade, served cold

Unless one has restaurant facilities and plenty of kitchen help, I think a hot green vegetable is very difficult to serve successfully to a large group. I will always opt, instead, for a copious vegetable salad or something like the platter of cold cooked and marinated vegetables suggested here. They look attractive, they taste good, and since there will also be a fresh green salad on the table, I don't think you need more than a piece or 2 of each vegetable per serving, plus a spoonful of mushrooms.

The idea here is to make a communal cooking bath of spiced liquid, and to cook each batch of vegetables separately in the bath, each for its allotted time. Finally you reduce the liquid to an essence, and baste the vegetables with the resulting sauce—with the exceptions of the bright-green vegetables, which are treated differently, as you will see.

For 10 people

Spiced Cooking Liquid à la Grecque: *6 cups (1½ L)*
1 cup (¼ L) thinly sliced onions
⅓ cup (¾ dL) olive oil
6 cups (1½ L) water
The zest of 1 lemon (yellow part of peel removed with a vegetable peeler)
4 Tb fresh lemon juice
⅛ tsp each mustard seeds, coriander, and saffron threads
½ tsp fennel seeds
8 peppercorns
8 to 10 parsley stems (not the leaves)
2 cloves garlic, crushed with their peel
1 tsp salt

For the Vegetable Platter:

Your choice of vegetables

Lemon juice

Fresh olive oil

Salt and freshly ground pepper

Parsley

Equipment:

A wide stainless-steel or enamel saucepan, casserole, or chicken fryer for cooking the vegetables; a skimmer or slotted spoon; various containers, such as glass baking dishes, to hold the marinating vegetables; 1 or several large platters to hold the finished product

Preparing the cooking liquid

Simmer the sliced onions for 6 to 8 minutes in the olive oil until tender and translucent, then add the rest of the ingredients and simmer slowly, covered, for 20 minutes. Drain through a sieve into another saucepan, pressing juices out of ingredients.

🕐 May be cooked a day or 2 in advance.

Small White Onions:

20 to 30

For easy peeling, drop the onions in a pan of boiling water, bring to the boil again, and boil 1 minute. Drain, shave off tops and bottoms, and slip off the skins. Stab a cross ¼ inch (¾ cm) deep in the root ends with the point of a small knife—to minimize their bursting while cooking. Drop into the cooking liquid, cover, and simmer slowly 20 to 30 minutes or until just tender. Remove with a slotted spoon and spread in a dish.

🕐 May be cooked a day or 2 in advance.

Zucchini and Yellow Summer Squash:

3 or 4 of each

Slice off the 2 ends, scrub the vegetables, and cut into crosswise chunks of about 1 inch (2.5 cm). Toss with 1 teaspoon salt and let drain for 20 minutes to rid them of excess moisture. Bring cooking liquid to the boil and drop in the vegetables; bring rapidly back to the boil and cook about 2 minutes, until barely cooked—still slightly crunchy. Drain and spread in a dish. (Zucchini and other summer squash need attention—too much cooking and they wilt, too little and they do not absorb the sauce.)

🕐 Best cooked the day of the dinner.

A sunburst of fresh vegetables à la grecque ready for the buffet table

Mushrooms:

1 quart (1 L)

Trim stem ends off mushrooms, drop the mushrooms into a large bowl of cold water, swish about, and drain immediately. Quarter or halve them if large, leave whole if small. Bring cooking liquid to the boil, drop in the mushrooms, and boil slowly for about 1 minute until barely cooked. Drain; place in a bowl.

    May be cooked a day in advance.

Cauliflower:

Cut the head into flowerettes and peel the stems; cook as in the directions for mushrooms.

    May be cooked a day in advance.

Leeks and Celery:

These always taste better than they look under such circumstances. You would use just the white part of the leeks, splitting it to remove any sand, then quartering or halving it after cooking. Cut celery stalks into 3-inch (8-cm) lengths about ½ inch (1½ cm) wide. Leeks need about 15 minutes of simmering; celery, about 10.

    May be cooked a day in advance.

Topinambours or Jerusalem Artichokes:

Scrub and simmer whole in the boiling liquid for about 30 minutes. Peel after cooking.

    May be cooked a day in advance.

Carrots:

Particularly attractive for their color, carrots are successful candidates because they do not get mushy. Select really fresh and flavorful baby carrots, or trim mature carrots into attractive small-carrot shapes; peel them before cooking. Simmer about 10 minutes in the liquid, until just tender but still with texture.

    May be cooked a day in advance.

Green Beans:

Green beans will discolor if cooked in the spiced liquid. Trim them, leave them whole, and cook in a large kettle of rapidly boiling salted water until barely tender. Drain, and refresh in cold water to stop the cooking and to set color and texture. Chill them, and toss in the reduced cooking liquid (below) 5 to 10 minutes before serving.

    Best cooked the day of the dinner.

Broccoli:

The same treatment goes for broccoli. Cut into flowerettes and peel stems; blanch in a large kettle of rapidly boiling salted water for 3 to 4 minutes only; drain; spread out in 1 layer to cool. Chill, and dress just before serving.

    Best cooked the day of the dinner.

Reducing the Cooking Liquid to a Sauce:

When all the vegetables are done, boil the cooking liquid down rapidly to about 1 cup (¼ L), and carefully correct seasoning.

Dressing the Vegetables:

Spoon a bit of the sauce over the onions, squash, and mushrooms, as well as the cauliflower, leeks, celery, topinambours, and carrots, if you are using them. Let marinate in the refrigerator for several hours. Dress the beans and broccoli shortly before serving. And just before serving, freshen all vegetables with drops of fresh lemon juice, olive oil, salt, freshly ground pepper, and sprigs or a mince of parsley where needed.

Tossed Green Salad

You may trim and wash the greens the day before, spin them dry, and store in plastic bags. Vinaigrette dressing suggestions are on page 111, including 1 for quantity occasions. Make the dressing in the morning, but dress the salad only at the last minute, eating samples to be sure there is enough dressing and that the seasoning is perfect. (Too often a party salad is not carefully tasted by the cook, and the result is disappointing.)

Orange Bavarian Torte

Molded liqueur-soaked cake layered with Bavarian cream; whipped cream and glazed orange peel topping

For a large party you certainly want a delicious as well as spectacular dessert that needs no last-minute fussing—something like a molded concoction or a cake. The torte described here is a handsome example, with its snowy mountain of whipped cream and pretty strands of glazed orange.

Although the recipe looks long, it consists only of cake that is split into horizontal layers, each of which is flavored with orange syrup, spread with Bavarian cream, and molded in a spring-form pan (or soufflé mold). Bavarian cream is simply a custard sauce made light with beaten egg whites, enriched with a modest amount of whipped cream, and given staying power with gelatin. The torte can be assembled several days before your party, or you can even make it and freeze it; you complete the final decoration the morning of the party.

Manufacturing Notes:

A *spring-form mold* is what I've suggested here because it is convenient to use in this type of recipe. But if you don't have one you can adapt the system to a soufflé mold, or even to a casserole lined with wax paper.

The cake layers. The easiest way to form the torte is to have a cake or cakes the diameter of your mold, and slice horizontally into layers as illustrated, next page. On the other hand, you can cut and patch any size of cake to make layers; your surgery will never show because all is covered by frosting when the torte is served.

When I bake my own, I double the proportions for a 3-egg yellow cake, such as the one for *génoise* on page 487 of *Mastering II*,

which fills my spring-form pan by about a third. I have to bake 2 cakes this way to have enough for the Bavarian torte. (Once I tried tripling the recipe instead, to save myself baking 2 cakes, but though the triple-recipe cake looked fine as it emerged from the oven, when sliced horizontally, the center core hadn't cooked through—it was a wet mass of batter.)

How much filling to make. I believe in having more rather than less, and the proportions for the Bavarian cream here will give you about 12 cups (3 quarts or 2¾ L), which will probably be more than you need since the spring-form has a capacity of 4 quarts (3¾ L). However, you can always make the torte higher by pinning a collar of foil around the rim of the pan. Or you can make yourself a little molded dessert out of the excess; store it in the freezer and you'll have something nice on hand for unexpected guests.

Strawberry sauce adds its tart fresh taste to this gorgeous torte.

The Cake:
10-by-3-inch (25-by-8-cm), serving 12 to 16 people

2 round cakes about 10 by 1 inches or 25 by 2.5 cm (see preceding notes)

The Orange Bavarian Cream:
12 cups or 3 quarts (2¾ L)

The grated rind of 3 oranges

1 cup (¼ L) strained fresh orange juice

4½ Tb (4½ envelopes) plain unflavored gelatin

12 egg yolks

1½ cups (9½ ounces or 275 g) sugar

2¼ cups (5½ dL) milk, heated in a small saucepan

1 Tb pure vanilla extract (optional)

8 egg whites (1 cup or ¼ L)

½ tsp cream of tartar and ⅛ tsp salt

3 Tb additional sugar

¾ cup (1¾ dL) heavy cream

3 Tb orange liqueur (or concentrated frozen orange juice, defrosted)

The Orange Liqueur Syrup:

1 cup (¼ L) water

½ cup (100 g) sugar

4 to 5 Tb orange liqueur (or concentrated frozen orange juice)

The Whipped Cream Frosting and Accompanying Sauce:

3 cups (¾ L) heavy cream

About ½ cup (70 g) sifted confectioners sugar

1 Tb pure vanilla extract

3 Tb orange liqueur

Decorative suggestions: candied orange peel or storebought kumquats in syrup cut into strips or designs

Sauce suggestions: sliced fresh strawberries flavored with sugar and a little orange liqueur, or a purée of sieved raspberries, or sliced oranges

Equipment:

A 10-by-3-inch (25-by-8-cm) spring-form pan (or other choices as noted earlier); wax paper; a stainless-steel 2-quart (2-L) saucepan for the custard; beating equipment for the egg whites; a giant-sized rubber spatula for easy folding; a bowl of ice cubes; a large metal bowl for whipping the cream; a round platter or board for serving the torte; a flexible-blade spatula and pastry bag with star tube for decorating

Preliminaries

Dot inside of spring-form mold with butter; cut a round of wax paper to fit the bottom and a strip to fit around the inside wall, and press them in place (butter will hold them there). Split the cakes, or cut to fit mold; you should have 3 or 4 layers; wrap in plastic to keep them from drying out. Grate the orange rind into a small saucepan, pour in the orange juice, and sprinkle the gelatin on top to soften. Make the orange sugar syrup: heat the water and sugar in another small pan; when sugar has completely dissolved, remove from heat and stir in the liqueur; cover and set aside.

Custard Sauce — Crème Anglaise:

Place the egg yolks in the stainless-steel saucepan. Using a wire whip, beat in the sugar by 2-tablespoon dollops with 3 to 4 seconds of beating between additions; continue beating for 2 to 3 minutes until mixture has thickened slightly. With a wire whip beat in the warm milk by driblets. Set over moderate heat and

Slice each cake in half horizontally to make four layers.

stir not too fast with a wooden spoon, reaching all over bottom of pan as custard slowly heats through. Watch carefully that you are not heating the sauce too fast or the yolks will turn granular; keep testing with your finger. When sauce is almost too hot, it is almost ready. Also watch surface of sauce: at first small foamy bubbles collect there, and as they begin to subside the sauce is almost ready. Finally, keep your eye alert for a wisp of steamy vapor rising from the pan—this, again, is an indication that the sauce is almost thickened. Keep on cooking slowly and stirring until the sauce is thick enough to coat the surface of the spoon as illustrated—if you overheat it, the egg yolks will curdle, but you must heat it enough to thicken. (Time: 5 to 8 minutes in all.)

Immediately remove from heat and continue stirring for a minute to stop the cooking. Stir in the vanilla, if you are using it.

🕐 May be cooked a day in advance, and needs no reheating before you continue.

Completing the Bavarian Cream:

(Once the Bavarian cream with its gelatin is completed you must go on to finish the torte or the cream will congeal.)

The gelatin. Set pan with orange and gelatin over moderate heat for a moment, stirring, to dissolve the gelatin completely: look closely to be sure there are no unmelted granules. By dribbles stir the gelatin into the custard.

The egg whites. Set beating bowl with egg whites over hot water for a moment to take off their chill, then start beating at slow speed. When foaming, in a minute or 2, beat in the cream of tartar and salt, and gradually increase speed to fast. When egg whites form soft peaks, beat in the additional sugar by spoonfuls, and continue beating for a few seconds until egg whites form stiff shining peaks. Fold the custard (warm or cold) into the egg whites.

Preliminary chilling. Set the custard bowl in a bowl of ice cubes (with water to cover them), and fold with the giant spatula several times, repeating almost every minute and reaching all around edge of bowl to draw cold custard from outside into the center. When center tests cool (but not chilled) to your finger, remove from ice.

Whipping and folding in the cream. Pour the ¾ cup (1¾ dL) cream into the metal bowl and whip over ice until the cream holds its shape softly. Fold into the cool custard, ending with the 3 tablespoons orange liqueur. Plan to assemble the torte at once, before the Bavarian cream starts to set. (But if by chance that does happen, fold gently over warm water just until it loosens.)

Assembling the torte

Place a layer of cake, cut side up, in the form, and baste with several spoonfuls of syrup. Ladle on a layer of Bavarian cream and top with a cake layer, cut side up. Baste with syrup, ladle on more cream, and, if there is room, make another layer. (You may have more Bavarian cream than you need; see notes preceding recipe.) Turn the final cake layer cut side up on

Custard sauce is done when it coats the spoon.

Fold whipped cream into cool (not chilled) custard.

your work surface, baste with syrup, and place, cut side down, over the final layer of Bavarian cream. Cover with plastic wrap and refrigerate for at least 6 hours to be sure the Bavarian cream and the torte itself have firmly set.

🕐   May be arranged 2 or 3 days in advance; may be frozen.

Note: If you are making more than 1 torte, and you have only 1 spring-form, wait for several hours until torte has set, then you can release the form. Slide the torte onto its serving platter or board, but keep the wax paper strip around the side of the cake; cover with a sheet of plastic wrap.

Decorating and serving

Whip the 3 cups (¾ L) cream over ice until quite firm, and it holds in fairly stiff peaks. Sift on and fold in sugar to taste, and droplets of vanilla and orange liqueur—but do not loosen the cream too much. Slip wax paper strips under edge of torte (so as not to mess up serving dish), and spread cream over top and around side of cake with flexible-blade spatula, saving enough for decorative swirls, which you will make with your pastry bag and star tube. Decorate with strands of glazed orange peel, kumquat, or whatever you have chosen.

🕐   Cake may be decorated several hours before serving. Keep chilled.

Cut like a regular cake, and serve the sauce on the side, or pass it separately.

Spreading the luscious Bavarian cream over liqueur-soaked cake layer

🕐 *Timing*

It's probably a good idea to read this chapter through, noting anything you find useful, and make out your own shopping and cooking schedule, spreading it out over several days. Since some of the dishes can be prepared well in advance, you have a good deal of flexibility. All I can provide here are a few mileposts.

An hour before the party, arrange your vegetable platter; but refrigerate it until you present the green salad. If you have only 1 oven, bake the gnocchi now, since they keep warm better than the *pissaladière*. When they're done, raise the oven setting, wait till oven heat is up, and bake the *pissaladière*, first opening and distributing the anchovies. Just about now (an hour before) you can reheat the beef, in the oven if you have 2, otherwise on the stove top, and keep warm. It only takes moments to rewarm the sausages, and they keep well over mild heat, so do it when you like. This is also true of the white beans.

Note: If you own, or can borrow, a slow cooker to warm the beans, your only dirty dish so far is the beef roaster. Refrigerator containers are all small enough for the dishwasher—and, now that their space is vacated, you can put Champagne in the refrigerator in good time for dessert. Jug white wines, of course, take longer to chill: do them in your ice chest.

The morning of the party: if you have enough saucepans and stove top burners, you can do your preparations in an hour. Cook the zucchini and yellow squash, the green beans, and the broccoli, for the vegetable platter. While the beans and broccoli are cooking, prepare the marinade and baste all vegetables except beans and broccoli. Next make your salad dressing; whip the cream and decorate the torte, then refrigerate. Now's the time, if you hadn't freezer space, to buy bagged ice cubes and store in ice chests; it won't hurt jug white wine to sit there for the rest of the day.

Note: Even on a gusty, dusty summer day, with all the windows open, you can set out your table well beforehand. Just cover things; some favor plastic cleaners' bags, but I find they grab at stemmed glasses and cause breakage. On flower arrangements: do them the day before, but in hot weather set them in a cool corner, out of the light; a wine cellar is ideal.

The day before: cook the beef, and finish its sauce. Prepare the salad greens and most of the makings for the cold vegetable platter: the onions, the mushrooms, cauliflower, leeks, celery, and topinambours. Now's a good time to set tables, "tidy all 'round," and fix flowers.

The day before that, brown the beef and cook it, and do the sausages and their sauce.

Two or 3 days before, make and refrigerate the *tarama brandade,* and cook the onions for the *pissaladière.*

Any time at all: make and freeze the dough for the *pissaladière,* the gnocchi, and the torte.

Vegetables may be trimmed and some even cooked the day before the party; beef may be browned the day before that.

Leftovers

If you had 10 guests, you're certain to have leftover beef, ham, and cake. Of the other dishes, all keep well except an already-baked *pissaladière* or browned *gnocchi*—tolerable rewarmed, both of them.

Sausage, beef, and *beans* are easily rewarmed: the sausage nuggets in their sauce, the beef ditto, the beans with added liquid if they seem dry. Puréed, the beans make a delicious soup—add broth. If serving cold, chill, then add cream, lemon, and herbs. A country *ham* will keep several weeks at least, well wrapped, in the refrigerator and is a wonderful resource— excellent in paper-thin slices as an hors d'oeuvre. Or grind scraps and add to sandwich spreads, stuffed eggs, etc. Save the bone for soup—split pea or bean preferred.

The raw *vegetables:* make salad, or cook and dice them for a *macédoine,* or mince them to garnish a consommé. *Vegetables à la grecque:* finish them off next day, no later.

The *torte,* refrigerated of course, will be delicious next day—or scrape off the whipped cream, and freeze the nude remains, then redress. Purée and freeze any leftover sauce to make a strawberry sherbet.

Mail-Order Hams:
I have used the following sources at one time or another:

Callaway Gardens, Pine Mountain, Georgia 31822
Gwaltney of Smithfield, P.O. Box 489, Smithfield, Virginia 23430
Jordan's Old Virginia Smokehouse, P.O. Box 324, Richmond, Virginia 23202
V. W. Joyner & Co., Smithfield, Virginia 23430
Col. Bill Newsom's Kentucky Country Hams, Princeton, Kentucky 42445
Smithfield Packing Co., Inc., Smithfield, Virginia 23430
E. M. Todd Co., Inc., P.O. Box 4167, Richmond, Virginia 23220

Appendix

Dough

Dough for Pies, Quiches, Tarts, Tartlets, and Flans:
For an 8-inch (20-cm) shell

1¾ cups (8 ounces or 225 g) all-purpose flour, preferably unbleached (measure by scooping dry-measure cups into flour and sweeping off excess)

1 tsp salt

1¼ sticks (5 ounces or 140 g) chilled unsalted butter

2 Tb (1 ounce or 30 g) chilled lard or shortening

5 to 8 Tb iced water

Equipment:

A mixing bowl and rubber spatula; or bowl and pastry blender or 2 knives and spatula; or food processor with steel blade

Measure the flour and salt into the mixing bowl or bowl of processor. Quarter the chilled butter lengthwise, cut crosswise into ¾-inch (1-cm) pieces, and add to the bowl or container along with the chilled lard or shortening, cut into small pieces.

Dough by hand
Rapidly, so fat will not soften, either rub it with the flour between the balls of your fingers until the fat is broken into pieces the size of small oatmeal flakes, or cut with pastry blender or knives until fat is the size of very coarse meal. (If fat softens during this process, refrigerate bowl or container for 20 minutes, then continue.) Then, with a rubber spatula, blend in 5 tablespoons iced water, pressing mixture against side of bowl to make a mass. Lift out massed pieces of dough onto your work surface, sprinkle droplets of water on the unmassed bits, press together, and add to rest of dough. Finish as in the final paragraph.

Dough in a food processor
The preceding proportions are right for machines with a 2-quart or 2-liter container; a large container will take double the amount. Turn machine on and off 4 or 5 times to break up the fat. Measure out 5 tablespoons iced water, turn the machine on, and pour it in. Turn machine on and off 5 or 6 times, and dough should begin to mass on blade; if not, dribble in another tablespoon water and repeat. Repeat again if necessary. Dough is done when it has begun to mass; it should not be overmixed. Remove dough to your work surface.

Finishing the dough
With the heel, not the warm palm, of your hand rapidly and roughly smear dough out 6 to 8 inches (15 to 20 cm) on your work surface by 3-spoonful bits, to make a final blending of fat and flour. If pastry seems stiff, you can at this time sprinkle on droplets more water as you smear. It should be pliable, but not damp and sticky. Knead and press it rapidly into a rough cake, flour lightly, and wrap in a sheet of plastic and a plastic bag. Chill for 1 hour — preferably 2 hours — before using, which will allow dough to relax while the flour particles absorb the liquid.

🕐 Will keep under refrigeration for a day or 2, but if you have used unbleached flour it will gradually turn gray; it is best to store it in the freezer, where it will keep perfectly for several months. Let thaw overnight in the refrigerator, or at room temperature, and then rechill.

Fresh Sausage Meat

For about 8 cups, or 4 pounds

8 cups (2 L) fresh ground pork — including 2 to 3 cups (½–¾ L) fresh pork fat or blanched salt pork fat — from shoulder, rib, or loin

1 Tb salt

1 Tb sage

1 tsp mace

½ tsp cracked pepper

1 tsp paprika

4 to 5 Tb white wine or vermouth

Optional other herbs: thyme, allspice

Grind pork not too fine in meat grinder or processor, beating in seasonings and wine or vermouth (to lighten the mixture). Sauté a spoonful and taste, then correct seasoning as you feel necessary.

🕐 Best made a day ahead, so that flavoring will have time to blend with meat.

To be used in the preceding scrapple, or to sauté in cakes, as breakfast sausage.

Salad Dressings

Vinaigrette:
Basic French dressing for salads, cold vegetables, and so forth
For ½ cup (1 dL), enough for 6

1 to 2 Tb excellent wine vinegar and/or lemon juice

¼ tsp salt

¼ tsp dry mustard

6 to 8 Tb best-quality olive oil or salad oil or a combination of both

Several grinds of fresh pepper

Optional: 1 tsp finely minced shallots or scallions and/or fresh or dried herbs, such as chives, tarragon, basil

Either beat the vinegar, salt, and mustard in a bowl until dissolved, then beat in the oil and seasonings; or place all ingredients in a screw-topped jar and shake vigorously to blend. Dip a piece of lettuce into the dressing and taste; correct seasoning.

Variations for Cold Fish Salads, Eggs, and Vegetables:
Garlic and lemon dressing

Purée a clove of garlic into a bowl, using a garlic press, then mash into a fine paste with the ¼ teaspoon salt and grated peel of ½ lemon. Proceed with vinaigrette as usual.

Vinaigrette with sesame paste
Make the garlic and lemon dressing, and beat in 1 teaspoon or so of sesame paste after you have added the lemon peel.

A creamy dressing
Make the dressing as usual, but also beat in an egg white or an egg yolk, or a tablespoon or 2 heavy cream or sour cream before adding the oil.

Tomato Sauce — with Fresh Tomatoes:

For use with meats, baked custards, fish, pizza toppings, pastas, etc.
For 2 ½ to 3 cups (½ to ¾ L)

1 cup (¼ L) minced onion

2 Tb olive oil

4 cups (1 L) tomato pulp (See Note)

1 imported bay leaf

½ tsp Italian or Provençal herb mixture

1 or more cloves garlic, puréed

Big pinch saffron threads (optional)

A 2-inch (5-cm) piece dried orange peel

Salt and pepper to taste

Cook the onion and olive oil in a heavy-bottomed saucepan, stirring frequently, until onion is limp and translucent but not browned (5 to 7 minutes). Stir in the tomato pulp, herbs, and seasonings, bring to the simmer, then cover and simmer slowly for 30 minutes, stirring occasionally. Taste, and carefully correct seasoning; if too thin, boil down rapidly, stirring.

Note: Out of tomato season, add a judicious amount of strained canned Italian-style plum tomatoes for color and flavor.

Index

Julia Child was born in Pasadena, California. She was graduated from Smith College and worked for the OSS during World War II in Ceylon and China. Afterward she lived in Paris, studied at the Cordon Bleu, and taught cooking with Simone Beck and Louisette Bertholle, with whom she wrote the first volume of *Mastering the Art of French Cooking* (1961).

In 1963 Boston's WGBH launched *The French Chef* television series, which made Julia Child a national celebrity, earning her the Peabody Award in 1965 and an Emmy in 1966; subsequent public television shows were *Julia Child & Company* (1978) and *Julia Child & More Company* (1980), both of which were accompanied by cookbooks, and from which the material in this volume is collated. Her more recent television series on cooking with master chefs and her subsequent books have only reconfirmed her position as the Grande Dame of American cooking. She lives in Cambridge, Massachusetts, and Santa Barbara, California.

A NOTE ON THE TYPE

The text of this book was set in Sabon, a typeface designed by Jan Tschichold (1902–1974), the well-known German typographer. Based loosely on the original designs by Claude Garamond (c. 1480–1561), Sabon is unique in that it was explicitly designed for hotmetal composition on both the Monotype and Linotype machines as well as for filmsetting. Designed in 1966 in Frankfurt, Sabon was named for the famous Lyons punch cutter Jacques Sabon, who is thought to have brought some of Garamond's matrices to Frankfurt.